In My Own Words

My Life's Journey
from
Beginning to Eternity

Inspirational Life Memoirs Written by
William Bernard Jones

Unless otherwise indicated, Scripture verses are taken from the King James Version

Marietta Jones
Editor

Tenita Johnson
Editor
So It Is Written LLC
Email: info@soitiswritten.net
www.soitiswritten.net

50% of sales from this book will go towards the William Bernard Jones Scholarship Fund.
WBJ Scholarship
PO Box 3553
Farmington Hills MI 48333
www.wbjscholarship.com

Printed in the United States of America

Dedication

This book is dedicated to the memory of William Bernard Jones, the author of the writings in this book. His mother Joyce named him William Bernard Jones, because while in the womb, she knew in her heart he had a special call on his life; he would either be a lawyer or a preacher. All those that knew him knew he was a little of both. There was a firm commitment in his heart towards God that he unashamedly shared with everyone that crossed his path from the prison yard to the roughest city streets of Detroit (Brightmore area). And he served faithfully at the Dunamis Outreach Ministries his passion for the things of God.

Bee (as he was known by his family and friends) also had a great love for his family. Bernard would often tell stories of how he and his siblings grew up and the respect he had for his mother raising four boys and a girl alone. His strength to contend with the many challenges he had to face was birthed in him during this time of his life. As he spoke about his siblings, you can tell that they were a tight bunch......THE JONESES'. Ernestine, being the oldest, was the enforcer; Michael and Prentice were his road dogs; and Damon had the swag. His nieces, nephews, cousins, and his Dunamis Outreach Ministry Church (DOM) family meant the world to him as well. A special thanks to DOM and Pastor's Reginald and Kelly Lane for giving him hope again.

Contents

Foreword

I want to share with the world the heart of a man that I loved, honored and was blessed to have known for 13 years; 4 as his wife. What can I say….I fell in love with my best friend! God used him to challenge, encourage and strengthen me. His life left prints on everything he touched. Whether it was dealing with computers to heating and cooling or the prison yard to the pulpit, William Bernard Jones loved life and every aspect of it and NEVER changed his confession about what he believed…..Jesus Christ is the answer!

Watching Bernard face challenges most would not be able to stand up against, I saw his strength as a man and most of all his humility as a man of God. He never made excuses for his challenges, but he tried to do all he could do to overcome the demons that tormented his soul. Even though his life ended, in what many would say was a tragic way, I know for a certainty that his life was not just about his love for Christ, but most importantly Christ's love for Bernard.

The author of these writings was taken from us far too soon. Bernard had a brilliancy about him that was unmatched by any. One of his greatest desires in life was to leave a mark on the earth, so that when God called him home, something of him would be left behind. As you read his heart, know that this is just a sample of what God deposited into this brilliant mind to share with his family and the world. Try to understand the heart of the man, because a book should never be judged by its cover. Yes, his life was tainted with seasons of struggle, torment, addiction and heartache; but his journey here on earth **DID** come to a triumphant conclusion, which continues now in eternity.

Marietta Jones

Introduction

Stop!

So many things movin' all at once,

attempting to overtake me, all with one punch.

How can I make all of this drama cease,

and be still, like the waters beholding their peace?

I need a release because things are moving too fast;

 a release from my mind's worries; this here is my task.

Am I running from me? Some would surely say.

But if they knew what went on in the inside, they wouldn't say.

What I'm in search for is not peace of mind;

something throughout my life that's been hard to find.

Until I met the man named Jesus, who did much more than I asked,

and gave me peace beyond measure that would always last.

So there's no need to look outside myself,

because Jesus is Savior and His Spirit, my help.

Beginning

March 11, 1969

My Testimony

And I heard a loud voice saying in heaven, Now is come salvation, and strength, and the kingdom of our God, and the power of His Christ: for the accuser of our brethren (the enemy is cast down, which accused them before our God day and night. And they overcame him (the enemy) by the blood of the Lamb, and by the word of their testimony; and they loved not their own lives unto death. (Revelation 12:10-11)

Notoriety isn't what I seek at all in writing what God puts on my heart. All that I desire is to do what He desires that I do. I do know in part that God has always used me in a way that hasn't been popular by many, and that has always caused me tremendous pain. But right now, I need deliverance, so I have to push through that pain and do His will in writing.

I'll begin by saying that I am nobody. But in being nobody, God said that He would make me somebody, and in making me somebody, that He would touch everybody that He brings me in contact with into His glory.

At this very moment, I sit here with a mind that is full of confusion, doubt and unbelief. These things have happened to me in large part due to sin and rebellion. But God has a way of taking things and making them work together for the good to those that love

Him and are called according to His purpose. Yes, I knew God and served Him with my entire heart, but yet and still, I fail away. My hedge was removed and I cursed God in my confusion and sickness. But I thank God that in spite of this, He's bringing me out. In bringing me out, He also allowed me to learn a great deal about the hearts and souls of His people.

I could write volumes as to what caused me to turn back to the world, but we already know those things. What I would like to note is what this falling away did to me and why it was so hard to be restored.

Due to choices I made, whether willingly or unwillingly at a young age, I spent eighteen years incarcerated. Prior to incarceration, I was already in bondage at an early age. I was introduced to drugs at the age of twelve by a man that I looked up to as a hero. Due to this habit, it caused a great deal of low self-esteem, rejection and even a feeling of hopelessness at an age where I should have been playing on a playground. I was ostracized by family, friends and even by myself. This produced, at an early period in my life, an attitude that said, "Whatever!" I was marked a long time ago by not only the devil, but by people, to be destined to be nobody or even dead.

I saw drugs, shooting, killings, violence, and dysfunction. This was a norm and it was okay with me. I was pretty much on my own at the age of thirteen. Not because I didn't have a family, but because I had Satan and he had me.

I found myself in and out of jail until one day I was finally sent to the adult prison. Here I was, coming from bondage to yet another level of bondage. Every problem that I had became larger. I hated prison as well as the people inside of it. I felt lonely, distant, scared, empty and crazy all at the same time. By this time, I hated my family more than I hated anything else, besides the prison guards. I had to live in that place with uncertainty every day as to whether I would live to see the next day. I often wondered if I would live to one day finally be somebody worthwhile. But nothing changed. I became bitterer and my soul's hole only became larger.

I had people praying for me on the outside while I was incarcerated, but it didn't mean anything. It was the same old thing to me. I was already witnessing people that only ran their mouths, but would never produce. So I became a militant, Black Nationalist, hateful man. At least now I had a way to vent my resentment. But I would later learn that this too was only a learning experience.

Prior to being released, I received the Lord in a way that was so real that I was convinced. I came home a man sold out to Jesus, with the desire to do nothing more than to serve Him. But now the hedge was removed and I would be tested. I learned fast that there was a difference between inside and outside in terms of the church and believers. I came home wanting to grow and serve, but I ran into Hollywood. I already had my own demons, unbeknownst to me, but running into the things that I saw in the Body of Christ only agitated those unhealed parts of me.

I came home to what I discerned to be idolatry in the church. Although the language was Christian, the spirit was something different. I was being asked to bow to Jesus, by way of bowing to the personage of a man (preacher). I made it clear early on that I wouldn't do this, so I was labeled early on as a rebellious brother. No, I wasn't rebellious, I was hearing from God, the same God that said, "My glory, I will not share with another." I saw unholy things. I allowed my family to be used by those who served their bellies. As a young believer, this was confusing. I saw the same game being manifested on the pulpit that I'd seen on the street corners and in prison with pimps, dealers and killers. Call it what you may, it was a familiar spirit, but I still saw it. I tried to talk with believers and leaders, but instead would only be marked as a trouble maker. Yes, it got to the point where I became a troublemaker, because I wasn't equipped to deal with this in the spirit because I was a babe in Christ.

I saw the church being used like the army, following their familiar slogan "**BE ALL YOU CAN BE.**" Church had become a place that was only a substitute for the nightclub, drugs and late-night booty-calls. I saw where people could not grow in the ministry because they didn't have immediate benefits (finances) to those who served their belly. I saw the way people and ministry names were being exalted over the One who lived, died and came back. I saw the way ministry gifts were misused and held up as an idol. I saw the way people would appear as if they had power over the way the Holy Spirit moved and performed in the lives of God's people. I saw what God alone holds and controls in His hand, being supposedly released by others. I saw the gifts of the Spirit being patented and monopolized by others who desired to keep people running to them instead of Jesus.

These things, in addition to my immaturity, were the beginning of my fall. Instead of calling on the Lord or standing with another saint in agreement, I started looking back to what I was familiar with--the world. When I did this, it thoroughly ripped me apart. I went back to criminal activity, which brought on everything that goes with it. Everything resurfaced--the drugs, alcohol, violence, unbelief, fear, doubt, resentment, not to mention all the pain I was causing my family. Lord, forgive me.

I spent many days in the streets, wandering, scared, and lost, without any care in the world. Many times, my own wife had to come and pull me out of dangerous territories. Thank God for a loving and believing wife. It was this very woman that God used so many times to comfort me and remind me of the love of a Father. Sin isn't worthy all you will lose and all that you will encounter! I spent many days in bed, being tormented by the multitudes of demonic spirits. Oh yes, God is much more real to me today. I spent many nights crying, shaking, pacing, and screaming, on the verge of losing my mind. Various thoughts of suicide raced through my mind. The only thing that really kept me from taking out myself was the Holy Spirit. Torment wasn't only confined to me, but it affected my wife as well. I had to seek counseling and take anti-depressants to deal with this. None of it worked.

Well God said, "Enough is enough" since I would not. No matter what, hold on to the unfailing hand of Jesus. Take it from someone that has lost a great deal of time and has experienced much pain; you don't want to go there. There will be many hard days, but in God, you will get through them. Learn how to believe God, look to God, have faith in Him and He will get you to the other side. People will change, but God has committed Himself to watch over what we commit to Him. In spite of all that I went through, and most was my doing, God has spoken again. This time, I'm going to do what He has been telling me to do for quite some time. Stop looking at my bruises and stains and look at the bruises, stains and scars on my Lord Jesus, and get on with His work. I'm low and the covers are off. God says to cry out and spare not and by His Spirit, I will do just that with His help. God has told me who I am and why He made me the way He has. He also told me not to say who I am, but to simply be the man He has ordained me to be. As my pastor (Reginald Lane – Dunamis Outreach Ministries Worldwide) says, we are not a band of apostles, pastor's evangelists, bishops, etc... God didn't say, "Let the prophets of the Lord say so." He said, *Let the redeemed of the Lord say so.* (Psalms 107:2) I am the redeemed of the Lord and He is the Redeemer alone.

In order to be able to love and care for the souls of His children, we have to be able to identify and even feel the pain of those He's sending us to minister to. There are many people out there hurting and living in terror. You see them and so do I. This type of work you don't get paid for. This type of work you don't get twenty men following behind you because nobody wants to go. We have to stop reaching to satisfy our hearts and satisfy the heart of God. You want to know where His heart is? It is where it has always been:

> *The Spirit of the Lord GOD is upon me; because the LORD hath anointed me to preach good tidings unto the meek; he hath sent me to bind up the brokenhearted, to proclaim liberty to the captives, and the opening of the prison to them that are bound; To proclaim the acceptable year of the LORD, and the day of vengeance of our God; to comfort all that mourn; To appoint unto them that mourn in Zion, to give unto them beauty for ashes, the oil of joy for mourning, the garment of praise for the spirit of heaviness; that they might*

be called trees of righteousness, the planting of the LORD, that he might be glorified.(Isaiah 61:1-3)

The above scripture clearly states why our Lord Jesus was anointed. Remember, our service (ministry) is to Him. Our service is an extension of His ministry, the one who started what we call "The Church." Are we ministering in that same Spirit and under that self-same anointing? Are we preaching to the meek? Binding up the broken-hearted? Proclaiming liberty to the captive? Opening the prison to those that are bound? Proclaiming the acceptable year of the Lord instead of man's year? Are we comforting those that mourn or just those that can afford tithes and offerings? Those that will praise and honor us as gods? As the Word says, *Examine yourselves, whether ye be in the faith.* (2 Corinthians 13:5) We judge ourselves by the Word, not by what others think and say. Let us be bold and daring, and judge ourselves by the Word above to the extent that we have judged others and see if we are truly walking in His Word. I had to do it and found out I was way off track. I'm dirty, but He is more than willing and able to make me clean.

Judge the word by the Word. Test the spirit by the Spirit. Stop being afraid like I was and challenge the lies of the enemy, the accuser of the brethren, no matter what form he manifests himself in. God is our judge and we must remember that. He alone will call us to account.

In Due Season

We understand that God works within His own timeframe. We also know that we can ask Him for something, and He will delay it just to see what type of attitude we will hold while waiting. He wants to see if we will continue to look to Him, praise Him and trust in Him for all things. It's not necessarily so He can see where we are because He already knows, but more so that we can see where we are in our trust in Him. Your prayers have already been answered. That blessing resides within the spiritual realm and we are only waiting for the physical manifestation of it. All things with God begin with His thoughts before anyone sees the manifestation of it. Know for sure that it's already been given. It's kind of like what the Lord told Habakkuk in 2:2-3, *And the LORD answered me, and said, Write the vision, and make [it] plain upon tables, that he may run that readeth it. For the vision [is] yet for an appointed time, but at the end it shall speak, and not lie: though it tarry, wait for it; because it will surely come, it will not tarry.* Well the Word teaches us to ask and it shall be given, right? If we ask according to His Word, He will give. You have to see the manifestation within your mind and continue to call those things into being that are not as though they are. Remember, we are walking by faith and not by sight. Our faith tells us that we have received those things we've asked for and so we should walk according to that. With the vision that Habakkuk wrote down for the Israelites, they didn't see the outward manifestation of it. That didn't mean it didn't exist, though. They didn't see the outward manifestation of it, but God revealed it through His spoken Word, which is very real. The Lord told them to wait for it, because it will surely come. Praise God for His Word. He gives us (the anointed) a glimpse to how things operate within the spiritual realm.

I have truly learned that our words really have power, especially when we are speaking words into our own lives and circumstances. I'm comfortable in my current condition, but I'm also speaking a word concerning it. Many people believe things, but they speak a different word. They ask God for things and when it doesn't happen the way that they have asked, they begin to question God. They ask God why His Word instructs us to ask and it shall be given (Matthew 7:7, Luke 11:9), yet when I've done that very thing, I still haven't received? They become distraught and disoriented. God doesn't want us like that. He wants us to receive our blessings in the spirit (spiritual realm) and wait for the outward manifestation of it because it's coming. It's just like a pregnancy. You don't see the baby, but you feel it on the inside. You don't see the baby, but you feel the pains on the inside. Before the baby is delivered, a mother goes through birthing pangs. At an appointed time, the child is delivered. We had to wait. We had to experience certain pangs. We had to allow certain developments to take place before we got a chance to see that baby being delivered into the world. We are believers and we will not abort babies being delivered into the world.

We don't see it, but we know they exist. How? *But God hath revealed [them] unto us by his Spirit: for the Spirit searcheth all things, yea, the deep things of God.* (1 Corinthians 2:10) Look deep within your spirit and you will see the answers to your prayers. Ezekiel 12:21-28 says:

> *And the word of the LORD came unto me, saying, Son of man, what is that proverb that ye have in the land of Israel, saying, The days are prolonged, and every vision faileth? Tell them therefore, Thus saith the Lord GOD; I will make this proverb to cease, and they shall no more use it as a proverb in Israel; but say unto them, The days are at hand, and the effect of every vision. For there shall be no more any vain vision nor flattering divination within the house of Israel. For I am the LORD: I will speak, and the word that I shall speak shall come to pass; it shall be no more prolonged: for in your days, O rebellious house, will I say the word, and will perform it, saith the Lord GOD. Again the word of the LORD came to me, saying. Son of man, behold, they of the house of Israel say, The vision that he seeth is for many days to come, and he prophesieth of the times that are far off. Therefore say unto them, Thus saith the Lord GOD; There shall none of my words be prolonged any more, but the word which I have spoken shall be done, saith the Lord GOD.*

The story speaks for itself, but allow me to cite my Bible commentary on these verses. The prophecies that Ezekiel gave about the coming destruction had been confirmed by his vision and illustrated by signs. But nothing had yet happened, and the people assumed that nothing would happen, or that if it did, it would be so far in the future that they did not need to concern themselves about it. They also concluded that they could no longer trust the true prophets. Now, God told them that what had been prophesied so far in advance would indeed come to pass, and that it would be in their days.

Throughout our walk with the Lord, we ask for things and often feel that He has heard our request and answered in the positive. When we don't see the manifestation within our timeframe, we question our inner prophets (the still small voice or our own spiritual confirmations) and say to ourselves that those true prophets can no longer be trusted. God tells us something and we wait to see the manifestation. After so many seasons, we convince ourselves that it wasn't God and maybe it was our own heart. We begin to doubt and therefore, give place to the enemy. Without a vision, people will perish. (Proverbs 29:18) Our visions must come from the Lord. We can have our own desires and have a vision formed through the Word, which encompasses God's will in addition to the very things that we asked for. Those things must be in accord with the Word and reflective to God's will for our lives. When He gives us those visions and the Word gives us confirmation that it is within the will of God, then we have to grasp onto that thing and press forward.

Brethren, I count not myself to have apprehended: but this one thing I do, forgetting those things which are behind, and reaching forth unto those things which are before, I press toward the mark for the prize of the high calling of God in Christ Jesus. (Philippians 3:13-14)

The word 'press' is interesting here because it denotes to impel; shove; urge; hasten; push; propel; force and pressure. This word also denotes that in pressing toward the mark, we have some things that will resist us as we press on. Objects of opposition create an atmosphere that demands that we do some shoving, forcing and propelling in order to get to that mark. We have to take it by force! What are some of the opposing things that we are instructed to press forward against? Some include doubt, fear, unbelief, demons, circumstances, anger, false visions, etc. The reason I stated false visions is because at times, we begin to see ourselves in ways in which God doesn't see us. The Lord tells us to ask anything in His name and it will be done. We ask, but if we don't see it after so long, we begin to see our prayers as being not answered; the devil is a liar! We have to continue to see ourselves through God's view of us. The Word says we are more than conquerors, a chosen generation, a royal priesthood, a holy nation, a peculiar people, children of God, blessed with heavenly blessings, and righteous. (1 Peter 2:9) We have to remember at all times who we are in Christ.

All I'm Trying to Say is...

What can I do to express how I feel?

And do it in a way where I keep it real?

My words are the arrows and her heart is the target;

"There you go again, see what you started?"

You started off right just to end up wrong.

Damn I'm getting tired of this same ole song.

Why is it so hard for grown folks to talk?

Unless we have agreement, the two cannot walk.

So I search for words day by day,

with a strong desire to see a brand new day.

A day that brings joy, laughter and fun

that you can be sure to see the next day, just like the sun.

But in searching for words, I still come up short

because I bring the wrong ones to you and it only causes hurt.

This kind of drama has lasted too long.

Now I find myself searching for what went wrong.

But that's another journey that will take me nowhere,

except to a land called "Pain & Despair."

So what can I do to convey what's inside,

where you can see me again and I don't have to hide?

Not that way again because it's oh so hard!

But Calvary is where you'll get your refreshing and a way to her heart.

Why is everything about Jesus? Because He is the way.

But this time, my son, you have to make the choice to stay.

To stay at His feet and basking in his love,

for the remedy you need, He provides from above.

Yes, it will get hard, but so is life.

But to perish with the world is a much greater price.

A life without Christ, you have no victory,

and that's what you're experiencing now, but you just couldn't see.

Jesus Christ has always been the answer for the world at large.

But, you have to make the choice to let His Spirit take charge.

To take charge of your life and even your words; and become a true manifestation of God's glory indeed and not just Word.

What she needs to see is power and not talk,

and this demonstration comes through your walk.

Paul said, "The Kingdom of God is not in word, but in power."

This is what you both need to get through the hour.

So stop searching for words and ways to get by,

and allow His Sweet Spirit to have a try.

And don't ever let go, no, not again,

because it's already been said, "you perish in sin."

Now stand up, My son, and brush yourself off.

Your sins are forgiven and you're no longer lost.

Just hold your Queen's hand and you take the first step;

They're ordered by the Lord you know, so you will be kept.

And the love of God that has been shed abroad in your heart

will sweep her away and captivate her heart.

So there's no need for words, but only manifestations;

manifestations of our risen Christ's power as your life's demonstration.

By Promise and Oath

Who against hope believed in hope, that he might become the father of many nations, according to that which was spoken, So shall thy seed be. And being not weak in faith, he considered not his own body now dead, when he was about an hundred years old, neither yet the deadness of Sara's womb: He staggered not at the promise of God through unbelief; but was strong in faith, giving glory to God; And being fully persuaded that, what he had promised, he was able also to perform. And therefore it was imputed to him for righteousness. (Romans 4:18-22)

God is saying that we must have hope, even when human reasoning tells us that there's no hope. When society, family and even church members whisper that things are hopeless, against hope, believe in hope. God has spoken a Word concerning your future. He's also saying that your faith must be strong because when it is, you will not consider what you see and render life as being dead. We must allow those things to cause us to stagger in hope, but in strong faith continue to give glory to God because He's in control. We must be fully persuaded that what God has promised us, as being of Abraham's seed by faith, He is able also to perform. Just in case you didn't get the revelation in Romans, He speaks again in Hebrews:

For when God made promise to Abraham, because he could swear by no greater, he sware by himself, Saying, Surely blessing I will bless thee, and multiplying I will multiply thee. And so, after he had patiently endured, he obtained the promise. For men verily swear by the greater: and an oath for confirmation is to them an end of all strife. Wherein God, willing more abundantly to shew unto the heirs of promise the immutability of his counsel, confirmed it by an oath: That by two immutable things, in which it was impossible for God to lie, we might have a strong consolation, who have fled for refuge to lay hold upon the hope set before us: Which hope we have as an anchor of the soul, both sure and stedfast, and which entereth into that within the veil. (Hebrews 6:13-19)

God is saying that He has promised us a blessed future. He wants us to be fully convinced of this to the point where He swears by Himself that He shall bless us. We must, therefore, patiently endure, not stepping ahead of God, but allowing Him to lead the entire journey. To convince us of this point and how much He desires to bless us, He goes on to give me an understanding of this from a human point of view. He said, *Son, just as men enter into a contract with one another and confirm it with an oath to settle a dispute concerning their promise to one another, I now do the same with you. I give you my oath; therefore, it's settled; you will be blessed!* The Lord says that His counsel is unchangeable. *Son, I'm not going to change my mind. Blessings will overtake thee.* Therefore, by the two things, promise and oath, we have been given a strong consolation by God.

Look at what He does next. To show you how bad He desires to bless us, He goes on to say, *Which hope we have as an anchor of the soul, both sure and steadfast, and which entereth into that within the veil.* Let me tell you what that says to me. Son, I want to bless you so bad that I not only have promised you blessings, strong faith, vision, sworn by myself to an oath, but I have also placed an anchor to your soul. In other words, He wants to bless you so bad that he's attached an anchor to your soul so you won't stray too far away. God needs you close enough so that when the blessings come, they will be able to overtake you because you are where He put you.

While you are waiting, many things will come against you. You have to contend with your adversary, society and even church folk. And the pressures of dealing with all of that will cause you to rock the way a ship does in the waters although the ship is anchored. Due to the fact that you are in the water, there will be a certain amount of shaking and tossing to and fro. However, you will only rock so much. You will only be tossed so much because this anchor that God has placed on your soul will keep you from moving too far away from His presence. So when the storms come, know and understand that God is there. Don't consider the situations and what you see in the natural, but look to the vision God has given you through His Word, because within that vision lays your hope for something better to come. Don't let the storms obscure your vision. And know that the blessing is coming!

Lord, why must I face so many storms before your blessings overtake me? Because just as Abraham patiently endured, which gave way to him receiving the promise, you must likewise because you are his seed. It will be those storms that will develop more patience and endurance within you. While waiting on the promise, you are renewing your strength. When the blessings come, you will need all the strength you have to carry what God has for you. With blessings comes more responsibility.

Can any good thing come from Nazareth?

The Lord was from Nazareth. When the people discovered that our Lord was a Nazarene, their response was, "What, can any good thing come from Nazareth?" What was it about Nazareth that made people think that the Messiah could not come from there?

As believers, we trust God for everything and we know that He is omnipresent. Where we are geographically speaking does not determine whether God is with us. What determines that is our faith and heart toward God. Before I got saved in prison, I noticed something about myself; I changed! I changed in a way that I did not even realize. Nor did I know this change was taking place. Keep in mind that prison is a small community. It's a microorganism of the world. Before I started hustling in prison, my attitude was generally like the average guy. I could relate to them in every way. I began to work hard for my dollar and valued the fruit of my labor, more so than I used too. I have a good business mind, so I have always prospered when hustling. I began to acquire more and more I was the man. If someone needed to borrow money, I was the guy to come to. People looked up to me and needed me all the time. I would hear my name called all day long, every day; I had more than I could hold. I would have to pay people to hold on to some of my stuff. I began to spend money like it grew on trees because it was constantly coming in; I never had to come home for money. The average guy in prison has about $15 in his account. I would always have close to $1,000 in mine. I got so accustomed to this everywhere I went that it didn't mean anything to me. I started talking to people different because everybody owed me. I became very arrogant and opinionated about others. I would look down on others who didn't have what I had. I felt they were lazy and always had their hands out. I actually felt I was better than others. I looked at them as pheasants. If you didn't have money or was not part of the circle of people that were like I was, you were not in my circle. People started telling me that I was arrogant and vain, but I didn't see this and to make the matter worse, I didn't care.

When I got saved, I still had my hustle in place, but my attitude began to change toward others. I was more giving; I began to help those who were less fortunate and feel good about doing that. It wasn't long before the Lord began to speak to me about hustling. It was wrong. I was overcharging people and violating institutional rules by loaning. In July of 2003, I gave up hustling completely. I have trusted God completely and haven't lacked at all in any area. He continues to provide. I began to work and make only $14 a month. It's not close to what I used to make, but I'm thankful to God for it. He taught me that if I'm faithful in a few things, He will make me ruler over many. To admit pride has set in my heart doesn't mean that I'm ugly; it only means that I was in need of a make-over. As I acquired a certain status in the prison community, I became so vain and arrogant that I couldn't see myself anymore. Pride is the hardest enemy to see because it blinds us, but yet other people can see it.

Pride made me lose touch with the very people that I myself came from. Regardless of how much I tried to separate myself from them, I was still what I was; a part of them. It made me critically judge others and render them unworthy; but I myself came from this very community in which I was not only critically judging, but also trying to separate myself from as much as possible. The more I acquired, the more I felt I wasn't like them. Can any good thing come from Nazareth? Yes it can and it still does. There's a verse that states: *Behold, the Lord's hand is not shortened, that it cannot save; neither his ear heavy, that it cannot hear.* (Isaiah 59:1) God's hand is long! He reached all the way into those ghettos and cities, such as Nazareth, and pulled out the Savior of humanity, and He's still reaching into those very same places to find His sons and daughters to be used as vessels. Here's a word that has always encouraged me....*But God chose the foolish things of the world to shame the wise; God chose the weak things of the world to shame the strong. He chose the lowly things of this world and the despised things--and the things that are not--to nullify the things that are.* (1 Corinthians 1:27-28 NIV)

But, as I stated already, this didn't happen right away. God allowed me to go up and down. He allowed me to experience both sides of having a little and having a lot. He allowed me to form views and attitudes that I would later have to re-visit, analyze and align with His word. Confronting oneself is not always easy and I'm a living testimony to that, but it's worth it. As Christians, we all have to one day "come to ourselves" the way the prodigal son did. Coming to oneself symbolizes the epitome of maturity. It ushers in change and it also represents a demarcation period in our life in which a line is drawn and we step from where we were into where God wants to bring us. The prodigal son had to struggle, though. His views were formed by his environment. His views became very warped but in his mind, they were normal and okay, until one day he found himself in a situation that was so appalling. This Jewish boy had squandered everything he had, so he hired himself out to someone for work feeding swine. He was so hungry that he considered eating the food that he was feeding those pigs. But the Word says, *He came to himself.* (Luke 15:17) How wonderful it is when we come to ourselves; it is a point such as that when God begins to really give to us some real "stuff".

The Measure of Success

Some people tend to measure others by their social and economic status, and view happiness or success through what a person has in material possessions, where they stay, who they know, and what they have. Jesus said that it would be hard for a rich man to enter into the Kingdom of Heaven and I understand why the Lord said that. Many people's perception of life is warped by what they consider success in life. Pride, in all forms, is destructive.

Condemnation & Fear

Condemnation will keep you in bondage. When we are under condemnation, we are really living in fear. When we are operating out of fear, we have actually cast out love (Christ). To be fearful is to be full of fear. In the Gospel according to Mark 5:35-43, I noticed that Jesus said to the ruler of the synagogue, *Be not afraid, only believe*. In other words, don't be seized with alarm and struck with fear, but only keep believing.

Prior to Jesus saying that, there were others in the church saying to the man that his daughter was dead, asking him why he would even trouble the Master. The enemy and others are always quick to pronounce burial rites over your situation. When we hear and take into account the report of the enemy and others, we allow fear to enter. Remember, perfect love casts out fear. So if we have fear, then that means the Word is not present in our hearts or we have allowed those weeds (evil-faithless) reports of others to choke it out. Jesus said, *Be not afraid, only believe.* I guess it's true that we don't stand on God's promises, we activate them.

We have to believe everything the Word of God says about *everything*! Anything not of faith is sin. Whatever our minds are saying we cannot believe unless it lines up with the Word. I don't care what we did or do, the Word says, *We have an advocate with the Father,* (1 John 2:1) so that settles the fear and condemnation issue.

Conquer and Control

When God created Adam and Eve, we read in Genesis 1:28, *And God blessed them, and God said unto them, Be fruitful, and multiply, and replenish the earth, and subdue it: and have dominion....* This is what God told us. But before He told us to do anything, He blessed us first. Remember that! God never asks you to do anything without giving you something first. He would never ask something of you if He hadn't given it to you because the truth is, you can't give anything to God that he hasn't already given you. Whenever God asks you for something, it's a compliment. What can you give God that He didn't give you? So He blessed them and then He asked something of them. He told them to be fruitful, multiply, replenish, subdue and have dominion.

God gives you blessings in seeds and tell you to turn it into fruit. Once you learn how to take something and bring it from seed form to fruition, the next thing He says is, "I want you to multiply it". Do it again, and again, and again. Then out of what you multiply, you can replenish whatever is lacking in your life. It's going to be replenished through what you're able to multiply. The next thing is subdue. The Hebrew rendering of the word subdue means to conquer. The fifth thing is dominion, which means to control. You cannot have power over anything in your business, family, and relationships until you conquer and control it. I cannot expect power to break forth in an area of my life that I haven't conquered; I will never get anywhere wishing. I believe God told Adam, 'I put you in this situation Adam. I put you in the middle of it, now run it.' He said, 'I want you to conquer it and everything you conquer, I want you to control.' If I'm trying to break through poverty, weakness, slothfulness, or whatever it is, I need to conquer it. The first thing I have to be able to control is myself. My blessing is in me and I have the power to get up whenever I get ready to get up and no devil in hell can stop me if I make up in my mind that I want to get up. I'm too old to be playing. I can't be forty years old, acting like I'm fifteen because stuff is breaking down all around me; I've got to replenish! I've got to replenish my children, family, and my relationships. It doesn't matter if all I have is a hut, I will sweep it out and keep it clean. Turn it into something and say, "God, see what I did with what you gave me?" God said if you are faithful over a few things, He will make you ruler over many. (Matthew 25:21) Where you may be in life may be just a test. God could be testing you to see what you will do with this little bit that you do have. If you take that little bit that you have and show God you can use it for His glory, He's going to give you a pressed down, shaken together, running over miracle in your life.

He said in Acts 1:8, *You shall receive power after that the Holy Spirit is come upon you.* I'm not supposed to be a Christian wimp. I can't be plugged up to all of that power and then faint! He said to *them that have no might that He increases strength.* (Isaiah 40:29) He said even the young men shall utterly fail, but they that wait upon the Lord shall renew their strength. (Isaiah 40:31) Awesome things will begin to happen in my life when I tap into the power. I have lived my entire life without being plugged up to God. I have done crazy stuff and yet still survived, made it out of car wrecks, yet still haven't lost my mind   God kept me alive for a purpose. God has something for me to do. I have put away all the symbols of power and symbols of success (money, material things, sex) and got hooked up to some real power, and have come to realize why I'm still alive. I'm not alive because I'm smart, gifted or good looking. The more I plug into God, the more I come to understand why I'm alive.

The study I have been doing for the past few months revealed some things to me that I want to share. This takes us to "exousia" and "dynamis". When Jesus rose from the dead, (Matthew 28:18) He said, *All power* [exousia/authority] *is given unto me in heaven and in earth.* Authority is a vested right. So I know as a man of God, that I have a right. This right was given to me by a sovereign God. I have the authority, or vested right, to function in the capacity that He has decreed for me. I can never do anything in the Kingdom that I don't have the badge for. The badge means I have the authority. That's why I study the Word of God because it tells me what I have the authority to do. If I try to do anything that I don't have the badge to do, then that means that it's illegal, and God won't bless it because I don't have the vested right. When there are things in a man's life where he is not exercising authority, it leads to depression and

45

obsession because he's walking around broke, pitiful and going through a crisis because he hasn't taken control of those circumstances. The Book teaches me that I have the authority to subdue. I can only conquer what He says is mine. If He says I can become it, then I can become it. So I don't have to look at my circumstances and say, "Can I do it?" I look at the Word of God and see if I have the authority to do it. If I have the authority, it doesn't make a difference that I don't have the money. I can get the money if I have the badge (authority). All of my life, I have been looking to the wrong stuff for power. I have been looking at my circumstances, asking my circumstances, "Can I do it?" If the Word of God says that I can do it, then that means that I have the badge to arrest that situation and say, "I arrest you right now in the name of Jesus." The reason I was never able to take control is because I wasn't plugged up to the real power, which is Jesus Christ. When I was out there, I wasn't hooked up to God. That's why things were not working for me.

In studying, I saw that the Greek word for power is dynamis, which is where the word dynamite derives from. It literally means power. Those two words (exousia and dynamis) can be likened to a police officer. His badge tells you that he has the vested right/authority to enforce law. He also has a gun on his side that drives that point across even more. The Word of God is exousia and the Holy Spirit is dynamis. That means, 'Devil if you don't respect the Word, then I'm going to loose the power of the Holy Ghost and everything fighting me got to move back out of my way'. Jesus said in Acts 1:8, *But ye shall receive power, after that the Holy Ghost is come upon you.* God gave me a weapon to deal with the forces of darkness out there. I don't have to use my old weapons; I can run off devils, I can rebuke powers by the power of the Holy Ghost through the authority that I have in the Word. Now when you got the Word, you got the badge (vested right/authority), but when you got the Holy Ghost, you got the stuff! So, just like that policeman, I'm packin' too!

If a person doesn't get a hold to some power and authority in the spirit, it doesn't matter what he drives, looks like, is built like, how well sexually he performs or how many woman he has. He's impotent and has no power!

Obedience through Suffering

I have been going to the Word of God seeking many things, such as an understanding of sanctification, consecration and His will and purpose for my life. I want Him to show me my heart and the impediments that forbid me from reaching what He has for me. I make it a habit to commit scripture to memory. The last few scriptures I committed to memory were 1 Corinthians 9:27, 2 Timothy 2:19-21, 1 Peter 1:6-7 and Psalms 1:1-3.

In studying the books of Leviticus, Numbers and Deuteronomy, God began to give me understanding of many things. Consecration has been heavily on my mind. What does it exactly mean? How shall I devote myself to this? Does it have anything to do with what I am seeking God for? Last night as I laid down to go to sleep after spending over an hour in prayer, the last scriptures that I committed to memory rose from within my spirit and came rushing to the forefront of my mind. In addition to the scriptures also came a story in Leviticus that I read, only days ago concerning sanctification and consecration. I meditated on every last one of those scriptures the way Psalm 1:2 instructs us to. From the meditation came revelation. God revealed to me what sanctification and consecration are and how it relates directly to me being able to have those other prayers answered and visions revealed. In Leviticus 8:1-36, the Lord instructed Moses to anoint Aaron and his sons as priest. During this anointing, they are also cleansed (sanctified). When you get to verse

33, they are instructed to stand at the door of the sanctuary for seven days in which they have entered into consecration. I thought on that for a moment as I lied in my bed and that's when it hit me; you cannot be consecrated without being set aside (sanctified) from. Sanctification sets you apart from distractions and consecration takes that separated person, quenching his thirst (giving him what he is in need of) in the presence of the Lord.

I then thought about the other scriptures that concern purging and keeping your body in subjectivity. Where do they fit? 2 Timothy 2:19-21 reads in part, *But in a great house there are not only vessels of gold and of silver, but also of wood and of earth; and some to honour, and some to dishonour. If a man therefore purge himself from these, he shall be a vessel unto honour, sanctified, and meet for the master's use, and prepared unto every good work.* I felt like doing a backwards flip. This scripture also made me think about what those impediments were that were forbidding me from receiving what God has for me. What's stopping me from hearing from God concerning these things? I asked the Lord to show me my heart and for Him to cleanse it, and whatever He desired for me to do about these things to tell me. He revealed to me that the pure in heart can see him. (Matthew 5:8) Therefore, I must purge myself and allow the Holy Spirit to do His part in the sanctification as well. What I'm saying here is that within sanctification and consecration lies the answers and remedies for all I desire to know, to understand and to receive.

49

The Book of Leviticus also reveals something of importance. When a man touches something that is dead, he is considered unclean. Therefore, there was a process of cleansing that had to be performed. Until that was done, the person was "cut-off" from the Lord. Dead things can also pertain to dead issues or unresolved issues. I remember the Lord telling me that prior to entering into 2004, He wanted me to let go of some things, things that hold me back from moving forward. I didn't realize how much God was really speaking to me at that time. He wanted me to let things go that should have been pronounced dead in my life due to my new birth in Christ. These dead things could be stopping us from experiencing the greatest move of God we have seen in our lives. If we cannot see God, because of all these unresolved issues, then how can we see God? In the scripture that says, *Blessed are the pure in heart, For they shall see God*, the word pure means to clean out. What God desires to reveal to us is worth the cleaning out.

Sometimes you can search and search, and it seems as if you haven't made any progress. You thought He would have moved by now! We stand glancing at our watch and thinking "Where is God?" But God doesn't synchronize His clock by our mortal watches. He has a set time to bless us; we have to just hold on. This brings me to Habakkuk 2:2: *And the LORD answered me, and said, Write the vision, and make it plain upon tables, that he may run that readeth it.* We have to stand firm, knowing His blessings and these visions He has given us are on the way. Great growth doesn't come when we are at the highest point in our life. Great growth comes through the valleys and low places where we feel vulnerable. The time God is really moving in our lives may seem to be the lowest moment we've ever experienced. Most believers believe that God works when the blessings come. That's not true! God is working on you, your faith and your character, when the blessing is delayed! The blessing is the reward that comes after you learn obedience through things you suffered (for Christ's sake) while waiting for it.

Purpose in Our Suffering

I And if children, then heirs; heirs of God, and joint-heirs with Christ; if so be that we suffer with [him], that we may be also glorified together. For I reckon that the sufferings of this present time [are] *not worthy* [to be compared] *with the glory which shall be revealed in us.* Romans 8:17-18

We suffer sometimes when doing what the Word instructs us to do. We suffer when we make certain decisions in life. But understand that this is an expected part of our walk with Christ and that glory days are ahead of us. God is showing us that there may be discomfort, but there is a light ahead. It's nice to know that in the midst of our suffering, there is meaning to it and relief to come soon as well. We cannot be hard on ourselves when we suffer, but instead we have to learn how to rejoice in that suffering because it's just an indicator that we are on our way.

Dreams & Visions

I was confused about the difference between vision and dreams, but today my understanding is much clearer. Dreams are visions. Not all dreams, but some dreams. For those dreams that are visions, God will give you discernment when you seek Him. Visions can come in a multitude of ways and dreams are one. I went through my concordance and could not find one scripture in which the devil entered into someone's dream. However, I did find a multitude of scriptures showing where God has and does. I used to think that if I woke up feeling afraid, then my dream wasn't from God. I was wrong.

Nebuchadnezzar had a dream in which he said he woke up troubled and afraid due to his dream. (Daniel 2:1) But we know that the Word says that the devil was cast from heaven into hell. (Luke 10:18) He no longer has access to the heavenly realm. He cannot operate within the spiritual realm; however, he can operate within the soulish realm. We are taught that the word 'soul' comes from the Greek word 'psyche', which refers to the mind. I believe that the enemy also infiltrates our minds through dreams at times. This accounts for dreams that are full of wickedness. I believe he tries to implant immoral thoughts within our subconscious because he knows *as a man thinketh in his heart, so is he.* (Proverbs 23:7) This is why the Holy Spirit renews our minds daily. I believe that dreams come from what is implanted within our subconscious mind. Bits and pieces are sometimes mixed together. That's why we have dreams at times that don't make any sense at all. Other times, we have dreams about things that we know we would never do. Other times, we have dreams about things that have been on our minds a great deal. Even some other times, God is warning us in our dreams, just as He did for Nebuchadnezzar. Every dream that seems scary isn't always bad. Just because the dream feels unpleasant doesn't mean it isn't God.

I noticed when I got baptized in the Spirit and spent a great deal of time in prayer and reading the Word, the enemy started attacking me through dreams. He attempted to instill fear within me, but the Spirit of the living God prevailed. When we experience dreams and it stands out extremely clear and continues, there's a good chance that God is speaking. We should always look closely at the details of dreams, asking ourselves what it means. When thinking of these things, also think of spiritual/scriptural principles. Remember when Daniel humbled himself and prayed for understanding? The Word says that his prayer was answered the first day, but the manifestation of it was withheld for twenty one days because of Satan. Is it possible that God has sent healing, deliverance, and prosperity, but the enemy is attempting to keep you bound?

Remember how the disciples tried to cast out a spirit that refused to come out? That spirit clung to that person until Jesus called it out. Something else also comes to mind. *For the weapons of our warfare* [are] *not carnal, but mighty through God to the pulling down of strong holds; Casting down imaginations, and every high thing that exalteth itself against the knowledge of God, and bringing into captivity every thought to the obedience of Christ; And having in a readiness to revenge all disobedience, when your obedience is fulfilled.* (2 Corinthians 10:4-6) The renewing of our mind is not always an easy process. It is often painful and full of labor. Could it be that words are being spoken that challenge you to pull down, pull out, and cast away some thoughts, ways, attitudes and views that you hold? But your natural mind is attempting to resist change in that fashion? The enemy knows that this change will lead you to your breakthrough. Remember, the enemy operates within the soulish realm--through our feelings, emotions, intellect, and mind. Remember, the mind is the battlefield. I heard a brother speak on this scripture: *Because the carnal mind* [is] *enmity against God: for it is not subject to the law of God, neither indeed can be.* (Romans 8:7) The mind resists change. Our spirit is changed and saved, but our minds and bodies are not. Our mind is constantly being renewed. This isn't to say that you are bad and not saved. God is trying to pull some things out of me and my mind tries to resist it, but God always wins.

In any case, whether it is God or the enemy, I do know this. Spiritual warfare is necessary. When I had my dreams, the enemy followed them up with his own. He tried to convince me that what I saw was not from God. He attempted to instill fear within me. Fear restricts and renders you incapable to press forward toward the high calling of God in Christ Jesus. (Philippians 3:14) Our prayer is that God reveals the origin to unsettled dreams. If they are from the enemy, then know that he's already defeated. If they are from God, we ask that He give you full confirmation that they are and an interpretation of what they are about. This prayer needs to be heartfelt where you open up your heart to God. This prayer has to be a warfare-type prayer. Put on the full armor on this one, calling out all enemies, demons and devils. Bind them all, whether they are the ones in the dreams, thoughts, health, relationship, or family. We are going to bind them by the authority that we have in the Word and command them to flee in Jesus' name. We are going to proclaim a complete healing in our bodies and minds. We are going to proclaim restoration of our families, finances, relationships, and freedom. Remember how Jesus dealt with the enemy in the wilderness by reciting the Word? When you pray, make sure you speak the Word in the presence of the devil. Make him scream, kick and run all the way to his final destination--hell! When this is done, begin praising God for all that He has done.

Get Untangled

The first step to all deliverance is our willingness to be honest with ourselves, others, and the Lord, and say that we are wrong in something we are doing, thinking or feeling. We need to admit that we need help. God resist the proud, but He gives grace to the humble. Grace is what will get us through. We have to carry our cross each day and be willing to take the wrongs and blows of others as Jesus did, without becoming combative.

I shared this with you because I love you. It's easier for a person to simply listen to you and "Amen" everything you say. But after that conversation, the wounds and issues remain. Be like the woman with the issue of blood and press in toward the Lord in faith. He alone can heal, deliver, and set you free. No seminar, preacher or person can do what our High Priest can do alone. *For we have not a Priest which cannot be touched with the feelings of our infirmities; but was in all points tempted like as we are, yet without sin.* (Hebrews 4:15) He knows your struggle and He alone has the answer. Take it to the Lord and leave it there. Claim your deliverance by faith and let those new deeds be the works and manifestation that he whom the Son has set free, is free indeed. Don't allow anyone to entangle you in the yoke of bondage again with carnality.

Going Through

I was told that the degree of affliction and trials that a person goes through is a sign of how big of a blessing and change that will ultimately come into his or her life. We have to look at the hard days in the way that God intends for us to. It seems kind of strange to hear a man say, *It was good that I was inflicted*, (Psalms 119:71) but after we come to understand why Psalmist said that, we too have to agree that it is good. It is good when you belong to Jesus because through those difficult days, you are moved closer toward what God intends for you to be, only if we look at this thing (trial/affliction) the right way and go through properly and learn what God has for us. If not, we will just go around the mountain many times. We should be willing to learn our lessons the first time around. We are no longer babes in Christ. We should have a good understanding of how He moves and develops us. The battle is for your future harvest, and the greater the battle, the greater your future!

Paul did not see the Kingdom in a simplistic way. In Acts, we see Paul pursuing the will of God, although he was touched by distress and persecution. In one instance, he was literally dragged out of a city, stoned, and left for dead. Immediately after that incident, Paul and his companions went throughout the region, proclaiming *we must through much tribulation enter in the kingdom of God.* (Acts 14:22) Here the brother is saying we enter into the Kingdom through many tribulations, but in another passage he says, *For the kingdom of God is not meat and drink; but of righteousness, and peace, and joy in the Holy Ghost.* (Romans 14:17) He was revealing a truth to us that would set us free from the fear of crisis and going though if we could understand it. Here's the truth. The kingdom of righteousness, peace, and joy is entered into by enduring tribulation with the right heart. This is how God uses what the enemy meant for evil for our good. If we can embrace this revelation, we will do more than just endure difficulty–we will flourish in it! Instead of looking for peace on the other side of the difficulty, we will gain HIS righteousness, peace, and joy in the midst of it. This is what I believe God wants us to learn, above all else, when we go through.

I Am a Soldier

We are soldiers in the army of God. The Lord Jesus Christ is our Commander! The Holy Bible is our code of conduct. Faith, prayer and the Word are our weapons of warfare. We have been taught by the Holy Spirit, trained by experience, tried by adversity and tested by fire. We are volunteers in this army and we are enlisted for eternity. We will either retire in this army at the rapture or die in this army, but we will not get out, sell out, be talked out, or pushed out. We are faithful, reliable, capable, and dependable. If our God needs us, we are there.

If He needs us in Sunday School to teach children, work with youth, help adults, or just sit and learn, He can use us because we're there. We are soldiers! We are not babies. We do not need to be pampered, patted, primed up, pumped up, picked up or pepped up. We are soldiers! No one has to call us, remind us, write us, visit us, entice us, or lure us. We are soldiers! We are not wimps! We are in place, saluting our King, obeying His orders, praising His name, and building His Kingdom.

No one has to send us flowers, gifts, food, cards, candy, or handouts. We do not need to be cuddled, cradled, cared for, or catered to. We are committed! We cannot have our feelings hurt bad enough to turn us around. We cannot be discouraged enough to turn aside. We cannot lose enough to cause us to quit. When Jesus called us to His army, we had nothing. If I end up with nothing, we will still break even. We will win!

Our God will supply all of our needs. We are more than conquerors. We will always triumph. We can do all things through Christ. Devils cannot defeat us. Battles cannot beat us. Money cannot buy us. Governments cannot destroy us. For when our Commander calls us from this battlefield, He will promote us, to a captain, and then bring us back to rule this world with Him. We are soldiers in the army and we are marching, claiming victory. We will not give up! We will not turn around! We are soldiers marching heaven bound! Here we stand. Will you stand with me?

It's Worth the Struggle

I have often asked God why He allows me to go through so much turmoil in my life. What I understand now is that it's not always the situation that God is trying to change, but sometimes He is trying to change us. What I mean by that is He allows us to go through so much in order to build up our immunity to struggles. Why? So that when He blesses us with blessings of abundance, we will have the strength to bear the responsibility of those blessings.

There are times when God will bless you and others have a problem seeing you blessed. Therefore, you have to deal with the pain of people you thought cared about you, jealousy, envy, and the hardship of managing all that God has given you. God can bless you with a big ministry, but with each blessing comes more responsibility. So sometimes the things we find ourselves facing are only a preliminary to building up our strength and endurance so that when those abundant blessings are given, we can handle them. So don't buckle under the pressure, but look at these trying times as a sign that God is simply trying to build us up because something good is coming.

I understand why Paul told us to rejoice in our tribulation now. He didn't say that only because we can count it as a blessing to suffer with Christ, but because the enduring of that suffering builds us up for greater things to come. Remember the scripture does say that our present suffering cannot be compared to the glory that is to come. Most people who excel in life and who are on top did not get there without struggle. Struggle is good for us all. No one can appreciate the enormity of our success if they haven't seen the ferocity of your struggle.

We really need to accept this process that God is taking us through because we are going to need the strength that comes from going through it. When God blesses and moves us out of the familiar, we will also face new predators. We will encounter new friends, but we will encounter new enemies as well. We must trust Him in new places as we did in familiar ones. God wants to enlarge our territory, so we are going to need all the strength we can hold to protect it.

Apply the Word to Life

The Word instructs us to enter into God's rest. When Jesus died on the cross and was resurrected, His work was finished. We don't have to keep struggling and suffering the way that we do. We have to enjoy life by walking with the Lord and resting in His finished work of redemption. I beg you, in the name of Jesus Christ, to be happy. I want you to hold your head up high and feel good about yourself. And know, not assume, not hope, but know that you are truly loved and will always be. Don't wait for the enemy to wage an attack; instead, keep him on the defense by constantly speaking God's Word concerning your life.

Maintain Your Victory by Walking In It

You walk in your victory by walking by faith. It makes no difference what the circumstances look like, feel like, or seem like. The reality of your life is what the revealed Word of God says. I encourage and rally you to stand up and endure hardness as a good soldier of Christ. Don't entangle yourself with the affairs of the world (worries, way of thinking, and handling your life as the world would). We look to the reality of the Word and not the circumstance. Let me share with you something about the parable of the feeding of 5000 and Jesus walking on water. Those jokers (disciples) sat in the boat for hours, attempting to toil and row against contrary winds. In all the time that they toiled, they still never made it to where the Lord told them to go. In trying to row against the contrary wind by their own strength, it also caused a storm to come into their lives. They still tried to overcome even in the storm by their own strength. However, they still never made it to the place the Lord told them to go. But when they saw our Lord on the water and cried out, Jesus stopped, jumped in the boat, and you notice two things happened: the storm stopped and they also got to the place Jesus told them He wanted them to go to. We cannot get there without Jesus. Never think that you have what it takes to do anything by your own strength. We live, move and have our being through Him.

The feeding of the 5000 says that if we put the little that we have (strength, talent, faith, etc.) in His hands, He will make it more than enough in addition to an overflow. First, compare Matthew 14:32, *And when they (Jesus and Peter) were come into the ship, the wind ceased;* with John 6:21, *Then they willingly received him (Jesus) into the ship; and immediately the ship was at the land wither they went.* We cannot get there without Jesus. We cannot get there without Jesus. We cannot get there without Jesus! And yes, there is great joy set before us!

One Purpose

Why do we hear preaching/teaching about things other than the love of Jesus Christ when it's only the message of Christ that matters? The Lord has allowed me to see ministries unfold on TV, ministries where God *was* moving tremendously. He also allowed me to see some ministries become misdirected by instead of preaching Christ, the messages have become people centered, feel good messages and about earthly prosperity. Oftentimes, you get ten minutes of message and twenty minutes of money-making advertisements. God desires to use us greatly, but we can't lose focus. Notoriety (or the desire for it) changes too many people. What's the use of becoming wealthy and yet, not being approved by God?

We all should desire to be true, devoted disciples of Christ by living His message in everything, staying within the perimeters of His Word and the leading of the Holy Ghost. All that we do (preach, teach, outreach, etc.) should be for one purpose--to please God! Preaching the gospel for profit is not an option for the believer.

My Heart to Yours

The first moment I saw you, my heart skipped a beat. Who is this mystery woman that stands at my feet? "Marietta who?" my mind inquisitively asked. Is this woman spoken for? I found out she was, but I didn't really care. There was something about her.

So I attempted to get closer, but only got so far. This woman is good, but doesn't know who you are. So I tried to use my street knowledge, to gain a point or two. But the Holy Ghost covered her. What was I to do?

This woman is spiritual, and I'm a slave to sin. But my game is tighter, I thought, so in due time, I'll win. But the more I tried to get closer, the more evident it became that her mind was going in a particular direction, and mine had to do the same.

But sins feels so good, and it's all I ever know! It's that kind of attitude, I thought, that will stop her from loving you. Where did that thought come from, maybe because I had heard it before? I didn't know then that Heaven had something greater in store. So I left that thought to itself, along with the woman I admired so much, and dated this girl called sin, that made me shiver with a touch. And in no time at all, this other girl would prove to be true, that the wages of your sins will catch up to you. "But I thought you loved me!" I said to sin in her face. What do I get from this relationship, besides sitting in this place? She said, "The wages of sin you surely know is death, so there ain't no need in calling me, because there ain't no love left."

So now I sit in a room, turned out and used, for chasing what I perceived was pleasure that left my soul bruised. All alone, being tormented day and night by memories called demons that left me with no sight. I called out to Allah, but didn't hear a word in return. There goes those demons again, "Burn baby, burn."

When the enemy had me to the point where I lost all hope, God's ministering angel appeared and simply said, "Hope!" Hope is not lost, if you turn to Jesus Christ, and the good thing about it is, He comes with no price. The price that was demanded, He paid with His blood at a place called Calvary. Now that's much love.

What are you talking about? And please identify yourself. I'm that mystery woman that you laid on the shelf. But here I am again, with the same message and intent, to share what I know about Jesus, hoping this time you'll be convinced. Bernard you don't need me, what you need is Christ. He will be everything you need, in this wretched world called life. If you would only stop torturing yourself, and blaming others for your plight, and call out for the name that's been exalted about all others, you'll get through the night. So she closed her letter, with a scripture or two. There I sat alone, wondering what I should do.

Confused and misguided, not knowing what to do, I didn't choose Jesus; instead I chose you. But with you being guided by God, and being filled with His spirit, the message I sent your way, you just wasn't with it. I tried everything I knew and became frustrated in my endeavor, and threw up my hands, and just said, "Whatever."

So a silent period came, and you were nowhere to be found. But little did I know that my change would come around. One by one, things began to disappear. I cried out for help, but no one was near. Affliction after affliction came rushing in like a mighty storm, but with each hardship came a revelation, and this wasn't a norm. I looked to others to help deliver me from this mess, but that's when the word came to me, "It's time to confess."

It's time to meet Jesus. That's what this drought is all about. And the wilderness is used to bring that about. You see, the Lord needs you broken with a contrite heart. The suffering you face son, will set you apart. Just the way I want you, all to myself, consecrated for My purpose and no one else. It's time for you and I to sit down and talk, and allow me to reveal through my Word, the way you should walk. So I confessed with my mouth, Jesus Christ is Lord, and was raised from the dead by the Father above.

As I took in the Word, a test would soon follow. And it knocked me to the ground, which made my faith seem hollow. What's going on Lord? I can't stand by my own strength. "Now you're learning my son." So a gift He sent, in the form of a rushing mighty wind, and cloven tongues of fire, that sat upon this young man and took my spirit higher. This is that in which was promised, in the latter days to come, "You are sealed to redemption; you belong to me son."

When I opened my eyes, everything was so clear. Endowed with power from on high, and the ability to see things as they are. The Word took on more meaning, so now I know who you are. I rushed to the water to be baptized in Christ. And when I arose from the water, I went looking for my wife.

I am a covenant child and Abraham's seed by faith. Blessed with every spiritual blessing that ushers me to a new place. The day that I stepped out of the baptism pool, I jumped on the phone. And to show how all things work together for good, you were at my home. Filled with the Holy Ghost, and the power of his might, being in your presence, was still out of sight.

The Lord reached down in my spirit and brought out something that had been buried for so long. A prayer that said, "I want this woman," and never felt it was wrong. So He spoke to your spirit and you sensed something inside. The next thing you knew, you jumped in your ride to see what took place. Has this man truly changed? Comparing spiritual things with spiritual, a confirmation you received indeed. God has begun a new thing, our spirits both perceived.

"Where do we go from here?" is the question we both asked. Let's keep acknowledging the Lord, who will direct our path. So we turned to our savior, with much prayer and fasting. And received the self-same revelation, "You've arrived at last."

Begin your journey together to become one. For your relationship in love will typify the Son, the Son's relationship that he has for His church. A love that's sacrificial and means so much.

So as we piece this union together, let this mind be in us which is in Christ. With every decision we make, we won't have to think twice. Let's not look at divorce statistics or what the critics may say. Instead keep our minds stayed on God, knowing He will lead our way. As the head of our house, I will be led by Christ and bring nothing but sweet blessings into your life. He who finds a wife finds a good thing and gains favor from the Lord. So together we sing; sing a new song, like Solomon did, because the birth of our relationship is like having a kid.

God has shed love in our hearts by the Holy Ghost which is given us. A love that's so divine that says, "In God we trust." So we both become an expression of God's love. So when we look at each other, what do we see? God loves you and He also loves me. The race is not to the swift, but for those that endure. The foundation of God forever stands sure. So as we walk together, in this divine union from on high, allow the image of the Son to be transformed to you and I.

A Fixed Fight

Our walk with Christ isn't a piece of cake. If *we endure, we shall also reign with him.* (2 Timothy 2:12) We are soldiers in His army. We will always be fighting (the good fight of faith), but we don't have to fight alone. Stop fighting alone and let Jesus and His soldiers help you in every battle.

Our Light Afflictions

I have often asked God why He allows me to go through so much turmoil in my life, even the things I've shared with you concerning the church. What I understand now is that it's not always the situation that God is trying to change, but us He is trying to change. What I mean by that is He allows us to go through so much in order to build up our immunity to struggles. Why? So that when He blesses us with the blessings of abundance, we will have the strength to bear the responsibility of those blessings. There are times when God will bless you and other have a problem seeing you blessed. Therefore, you have to deal with the pain of people who you thought cared about you stabbing you in the back, jealousy, envy, and the hardship of managing all that God had given you. God can bless you with a big ministry, but with each blessing comes more responsibility. So sometimes, the things we find ourselves facing are only a preliminary to building up our strength and endurance so that when those abundant blessings are given, we can handle them. So don't buckle under the pressure, but look at these trying times as a sign that God is simply trying to build us up because something good is coming. I understand why Paul told us to rejoice in our tribulation now. He didn't say that only because we can count it as a blessing to suffer with Christ, but because enduring that suffering builds us up for greater things to come. Remember the scripture does say, *For our light affliction, which is but for a moment, worketh for us a far more exceeding* [and] *eternal weight of glory, While we look not at the things which are seen, but at the things which are not seen: for the things which are seen [are] temporal; but the things which are not seen [are] eternal.* 2 Corinthians 4:17-18 Most people who excel in life and who are on did not get there without struggle. Struggle is good for us all. No one can appreciate the enormity of your success if they haven't seen the ferocity of your struggle.

God knows best and He's in control. God sees things ahead that we don't. While we are going through, He's always at work, doing things in other areas as well. When it comes together in His timing, it fits together perfect. God has heard your cry and He's not going to disappoint you. All of our faith has to be in Him, no matter what it looks or feels like. It's funny how He likes to make Himself known. He shows up and says, "I got this." The next thing you know, your hands are up in the air, praising Him for His goodness. Know in your heart that He's working, He knows what He's doing, He knows what's best, and He will show up.

Dents in the Armor

Sometimes, healing begins by admitting to ourselves that we have wounds. Oftentimes, we attempt to hide these wounds because we don't allow anyone else to see any dents in our armor. And why do we do this? We have postured ourselves to be counselors for others to the degree that we forget about ourselves. We have postured ourselves as such to the degree that others don't perceive that we also have issues.

Praying for Manifestation

And Elijah said unto Ahab, Get thee up, eat and drink; for [there is] a sound of abundance of rain. So Ahab went up to eat and to drink. And Elijah went up to the top of Carmel; and he cast himself down upon the earth, and put his face between his knees, So Ahab went up to eat and to drink. And Elijah went up to the top of Carmel; and he cast himself down upon the earth, and put his face between his knees, So Ahab went up to eat and to drink. And Elijah went up to the top of Carmel; and he cast himself down upon the earth, and put his face between his knees, And it came to pass in the mean while, that the heaven was black with clouds and wind, and there was a great rain. And Ahab rode, and went to Jezreel. And the hand of the LORD was on Elijah; and he girded up his loins, and ran before Ahab to the entrance of Jezreel. (1 Kings 18:41-46)

Not only did Elijah pray several times before he saw the manifestation of what he was praying for while on top of Mount Carmel, but there's something else interesting about this story when you back up and read 17:1 and 18:1.

And Elijah the Tishbite, [who was] of the inhabitants of Gilead, said unto Ahab, [As] the LORD God of Israel liveth, before whom I stand, there shall not be dew nor rain these years, but according to my word. (1 Kings 17:1)

And it came to pass [after] *many days, that the word of the LORD came to Elijah in the third year, saying, Go, shew thyself unto Ahab; and I will send rain upon the earth.* (1 Kings 18:1)

Elijah predicts to Ahab that God would shut up the heavens so that rain would not come upon the land for three and a half years. In 1 Kings 18:1, we see God told Elijah after three years to go and show himself to Ahab and that He would send rain. When you get to verse 41, we see something rather odd. Elijah didn't see any rain, but the text states that Elijah said *there is a sound of abundance of rain.* He sent Ahab to run out to the sea to check. Elijah prayed continuously for the manifestation of this rain and had to send Ahab back and forth several times to check for a manifestation.

I got many things out of this story. (1) When God tells you something, you can take it to the bank. (2) Some prayers are manifested immediately, while other have an appointed time. (3) The Word of God says that Elijah "heard" a sound of abundance of rain. He didn't see it, but he heard it. How can you hear the abundance of rain? I believe that he heard it in his spirit. God had placed a promise in his spirit in 1 Kings 18:1, and it never left him. Six months later, he clearly heard it in his spirit again.

Elias was a man subject to like passions as we are, and he prayed earnestly that it might not rain: and it rained not on the earth by the space of three years and six months. And he prayed again,

78

and the heaven gave rain, and the earth brought forth her fruit. (James 5:17-18)

After three and a half years, God opened the heavens and it rained. What am I saying here? God placed a word/promise in the man's spirit and there came a time when God caused a stirring of that word in him, and Elijah began to pray for the manifestation or birth of the very thing that he was impregnated with. He prayed with his head between his knees. This isn't any old kind of prayer. This man was praying as if he was trying to get what he heard on the inside to come out. He knew it was there because God had placed it in him some time ago. From time to time, the thought of it would come to mind, but there came a time when he couldn't get it off his mind because IT WAS TIME! I think that it's time for us to pray earnest prayers like that. It's time for us to pray that what He has placed within our spirits will manifest on the outside. Why shouldn't we? God has placed something in our spirits, also. I'm like Elijah; I cannot seem to get it off my mind. I hear in the daytime, and I hear it at night. What do you hear? If you hear it too, then let's get going. If you don't hear anything, then I ask that you believe others for their miracle and blessing and begin to pray earnestly. Elijah didn't quit in spite of the fact that God told him it would rain, yet he didn't see it. No, he kept going because he knew that was in his spirit. He knew what he was hearing and was determined to give birth to it. It's time to start praying!

God vs. Man

God doesn't place anything on us that we are not equipped to bear, but people will. Maturity of God's Word comes with time and experience. So at times, it is hard for us to discern the difference between God's will and man's demand for our life.

Relationships

Anytime a relationship is diminishing your peace and joy on a day to day basis, that's an unhealthy relationship. We know that all relationships will have their problems, but when it gets to the point where nobody is happy and nobody is willing to change or put the needed effort into making things better in order to get yourself back together, you have to sometimes sever your ties with others. That's painful as well because we become so accustomed to having someone in our life to keep us warm, happy and to give us that feeling that we are somebody, loved and appreciated. Real change is never easy and most of the time, very painful. You can't get to heaven without passing through your hell. But know this; once you come through this storm, there is a rainbow after that rain. At the end of that rainbow is a pot of riches. It may be him; then again it may not be him. There's a possibility that the Lord wants you all to Himself.

Never think that because you don't have a man in your life that it makes you unworthy, of little value or incomplete. When the Lord takes things away from us, it doesn't always mean that he did so because we are no worthy of it. It may mean that He has something much better. I believe that he has something better for His daughter. And like I said, it could be him, but a better him. Whatever the case, allow the Lord to reveal it to you. Don't let your emotions or body dictate to you what God may have for you. Why not? *For if ye live after the flesh, you shall die: but if ye through the spirit do mortify the deeds of the body, ye shall live. For as many are led by the spirit of God, they are sons of God.* (Romans 8:14) When we make choices based on our passions and desires, we are thinking in the flesh. This is why our relationships often die, because we live after the flesh. When we make our decisions based on the dictates of the spirit, we are thinking (acting) in the spirit. God said in the very beginning that it is not right that man should be alone. So He made him a mate. For this reason man should leave his father and mother and cleave unto his wife and they shall become one. So it's natural and within God's will that man and woman be together.

However, the Word also teaches, *He that finds a wife finds a good thing.* (Proverbs 18:22) Let God send you this man. Don't look for him because that's the man's duty--to find a wife. It's not wrong to desire a mate, but let your desire be based on your desire to want to become one (in spirit) with this man. In other words, I want a mate, but I want the type of mate that I can truly become one with and the only way that you can become one with him is by you having a mate that understands and knows that we are spiritual people. Spiritual people want to be led by the spirit. Therefore, if a man is in your life, he should be a spiritual person because when he is, he governs every part of his life with spiritual principles. If that man is being led by Christ, he will keep you happy because your relationship will be guided according to things of the spirit. Many times we look for a mate. But how do you look and what do you

82

look for? Do you want a mate to satisfy or gratify your sexual desire? Do you want a mate to take care of you financially? Do you want a mate to support you emotionally? You are saved in Christ, right? If that is so, then you have all you need in Him. Does that mean that he doesn't want you to have a mate? No, it doesn't. But he doesn't want us looking for mates for the wrong reasons and the wrong ways. When we become born again, we are new creatures in Christ; all things become new and old things are passed away. We no longer think the way we used to. We no longer do things the way we used to do them. We don't think according to the way that the world dictates to us that we should think. No, we think within the realms of a Christ-like mind.

The Word teaches us not to be unequally yoked with unbelievers. If you have a new mind in Christ, then in your desire you should want a mate that is like-minded. Once you stop thinking within the realms of the Spirit, you start thinking within the realms of the flesh. So you look and attract a particular element of people, you end up with a man who's mind is regulated by the world and not of God. This is why it is easy for him to commit adultery, abuse drugs, and not take care of his children. But, when you allow yourself to be guided by the spirit, you are able to discern and see these type of people for what they are. A person can tell you that they believe in God and are saved, but that doesn't mean anything. The demons believe in God and they tremble, but they still operate in rebellion. When you are saved and in a relationship with a man that's not saved (led by the spirit), you are doomed for failure most likely. Why? Because that man doesn't know you. We sometimes look at a person and think we see and know that person and within time, the true essence of that individual is revealed to you and you'll be like, "I thought that you were the one." We judged what we thought was reality (what was real) concerning that person, but we looked at them through our physical (carnal) eyes instead of through the spirit. This is why the book of Romans instructs us to renew our minds (way of thinking). This is the only way we can prove what that good and acceptable will of God is. The only way we can see true intent of others is by operating out of the Spirit. Like I said already, when you are with a person that's not saved, your relationship is doomed for failure most likely because your mate doesn't even know you!

Pay close attention to this: *For what man knoweth the things of a man, save the spirit of man which is in him? Even so the things of God knoweth no man, but the Spirit of God. Now we have received, not the spirit of this world, but the Spirit which is of God; that we might know the things that are freely given to us of God. Which things we also speak, not in the word which men wisdom teacheth, but which the Holy Ghost teacheth; comparing spiritual things with spiritual. But the natural man receiveth not the things of the spirit of God: For they are foolish unto him neither can he know them, because they are spiritually discerned. But he that is spiritual judgeth all things common, yet He himself is judged of no man. For who have known the mind of the lord that he may instruct them? But we have the mind of Christ.* (1 Corinthians 2:11-16)

When you are saved and operating with the mind of Christ, you are led by the Holy Spirit. When you have a mate that's not there, there's no balance in your relationship, home, life, or marriage. In believing in God, you have spiritual foundation that dictates that you live your life and every aspect of it according to spiritual principles. When you have a problem in your life, whether it's with the children or with your man, you solve those problems according to the Word. You know that it's wrong to commit adultery and if you even thought about it, the Holy Spirit convicts you immediately. When you think of doing wrong or think outside of the realm of the Spirit, the Holy Spirit convicts you immediately. With your unbelieving mate, it's totally different. His way of thinking is governed by the way the world thinks and what his flesh demands. This is why he can do almost anything and it doesn't bother him. As a believer, you approach your mate attempting to solve problems, but he or she can't seem to grasp what you are trying to tell them, much less care about accepting wise counsel. He doesn't know you nor does he understand you. You think you and that individual are very close, but actually the two of you are very far part. You try your best to get this man to understand you and where you are coming from, but he doesn't. And guess what, HE NEVER WILL. We spend years trying everything we know. We spend years trying to change them and bring them around, but nothing works. The reality of this is that you have a mate that doesn't know you, cannot know you, and will not know you unless he is born again. You can try everything you want to, but it won't happen. What you must do is open up your spiritual eyes to God's Word and go into the Word and find God's solution. *Eye hath not seen, nor ear heard, neither have entered in the heart of man, the things which God hath prepared for them that love him.* (1Corinthians 2:9) Keep your mind stayed on the Lord, and He will direct you in every way. I know it is not always easy, but it is the only way to TRUE VICTORY.

Something to Think About

Do you ever consider how fortunate we are to be called His children? He loves His children. Just think of this for a moment. In the Word, it says that the soul that sins must die. (Ezekiel 18:20) The Word also says that God does not desire that any perish. (2 Peter 3:9) We are the pride of His creation. However, just as David, we were all born into the world with a nature of sin; born into sin and shaped in iniquity. (Psalms 51:5) This appears to be a dilemma for God. On the one hand, He doesn't desire that any of us should perish. We are the pride of His creation. But He has said that the soul that sins shall surely die. So, when He looks at us, He sees what He loves, but at the same time He sees what He hates. He looks at us and sees the pride of His creation and sin at the same time. Justice demands that He fulfills His Word of destroying the sin sick soul. The enemy thought he had God. God wrapped himself in a body of flesh in order to reach us. He gave up everything to redeem us. He went broke saving us. He came from where He was to save us. He died and went to hell, and rose again so that we can be where He is.

Picture an innocent man who lived his entire life without sin and serving others. Can you see him? Now picture that man in the garden, knowing that the time had come for him to suffer a painful torture and death. The thought of what was ahead of him caused the human side of him to really stand out. The Word says He prayed so much that beads of sweat ran down his face like drops of blood. He asked that the cup pass from him. In other words, "Is there another way? I'll do anything, but this!" It had to be so because in doing so, He would also bear our pains and sorrows. This suffering that lay ahead of Him was tremendous. This was God in the flesh we are talking about. Now picture Him being lied on, mocked, spit on, and dragged through the street. He was made to carry the symbol of his death (the cross). After going through that, He was beaten, stripped, and nailed to a cross. He stayed there for what seemed to be eternity. When it was enough, He spoke His last words and died. That's not it! He went to hell so we would not have to go. He performed His work there among the unsaved souls. The power of the Word was so charged in hell that the Word says that bodies rose from the grave. Dead people were seen walking around Jerusalem. This is the true power of the Holy Ghost. Don't let anybody tell you what the power of the Word can't do for you. You know the rest--then He rose!

We always see images of Christ on the cross and pictures of Him with those pretty blue eyes. Those images give us a false impression of what God truly went through to save us. We are not our own. We have been bought with a price, the blood of the Lamb! God's love is mind boggling. His wisdom blows me away, but this is what He did for us so that we could be released from sin, guilt, bondage, and the power of the enemy. He didn't do all of this to bring us under the blood and allow the enemy to gain a stronghold in our life again. *He whom the Son sets free, is free indeed.* (John 8:36)

Therefore, I declare by the authority of Jesus Christ that we are free and healed in every way. We walk by faith and not by sight. Goodness and mercy shall follow us all the days of our life because He loves us!

At a Loss for Words

O clap your hands, all ye people; shout unto God with the voice of triumph. For the LORD most high is terrible; he is a great King over all the earth. (Psalms 47: 1-2)

Have you ever sat back and thought about the goodness of God, and then tried to find a word to describe that greatness, but couldn't seem to find a word? That happens because when you've truly experienced His greatness and try to describe it in words, it's often hard. That's why when Moses asked to see God's face, the Lord told him that he can see His back parts; in other words, His glory. When we get a glimpse of the Lord, it's amazing. When I think about what He's done for me, I reach for a word and the word terrible comes to mind. Yes, He terribly loves me!

Tell Them That I Said…

Keep looking to the Lord! Don't allow what you see going on around you, the whispers of the enemy, or lack of faith to convince you that serving the Lord is a waste of time. Continue to walk with Jesus. Continue to obey His marching orders. Continue to march around the city, believing God and very soon, some walls in your life will come tumbling down. I'm crazy for Jesus now. Nothing can separate me from the love of God, which is in Christ Jesus our Lord. Please convey this message for me.

I love you Momma.

And I give unto them eternal life; and they shall never perish, neither shall any [man] *pluck them out of my hand. My Father, which gave [them] me, is greater than all; and no* [man] *is able to pluck* [them] *out of my Father's hand. I and [my] Father are one.* (John 10:28-30)

Jesus said that those who the Father have given him, no one can pluck them out of His hands; that includes the enemy. So let me suggest a picture here. *Confirming the souls of the disciples, and exhorting them to continue in the faith, and that we must through much tribulation enter into the kingdom of God.* (Acts 14:22) and *Knowing this, that the trying of your faith worketh patience. But let patience have her perfect work, that ye may be perfect and entire, wanting nothing.* (James 1:3-4) You can never tell what God is up to most of the time until you receive your breakthrough. Every storm we find ourselves in is not always initiated by the devil. Some of those storms are placed in our lives for divine reasons, such as it gives us the chance to see ourselves. It gives us a chance to see the areas of our lives that need to be worked on. Those storms oftentimes move us to want to be alone. It's at times like that when we are able to hear the Lord loud and clear. The Word instructs us to *count it all joy* (James 1:2) when we go through the low periods. I think the reason the Apostle said that is because he understood that God is able to work on us best when we are in a state of vulnerability. Our God is a jealous God; He likes His praise. We will be allowed into situations that when we come out of them, we know for sure that it was no one other than the Most High Himself that brought us out. Sometimes, arriving at the low points in life are only an indication that God is preparing you for something and He needs you to acquire a particular thing before He takes you where He wants to; thus, so that you can be perfect and complete, lacking nothing. Remember, when God has a calling on your life, He will make sure you have all that you need to fulfill that call. Or it could be an indication that you are close to one of God's promises; just like there was a wilderness for the children of Israel before they received their promised land. Who do you think you are? You will have them too!

The Counsel of God

Believers, we are at a crucial stage in our lives, where we need to hear and seek the counsel of God like never before. We must trust Him for provision in every area of our lives. Whatever you are seeking Him for He will reveal it to you. So wait for that guidance to come. The Holy Spirit prompts us in a gentle way. You know how sometimes, out of nowhere, you sense a need to do something and that need arose from deep within you? That's how you know it is God because the Holy Spirit always works from the inside out, and the flesh works from the outside in. The counsel of God does not arise due to being provoked from something outside (flesh/world). Trust in the leading of the Holy Spirit.

We walk by faith and not by sight. Remember that when you are dealing with faith, the evidence of it is unseen. We step out, not based on what is there, but what is not there yet. We step out because we know that we are in the will of God and without faith, it is impossible to please Him.

Sudden Change

I speak the Word of God over our lives and every situation. We will live and not die! We will come through every trial and come out refined as pure gold. Our family is blessed now and any moment from now, we will begin to walk in the fullness of our blessings, in Jesus' name! I speak change into our lives right now; not tomorrow, next week or next year, but right now! Lord, we are going to be violent about this thing and not passive. We speak goodness, favor, and direction into the lives of our family, friends, and even our enemies. We thank you for this change, increase, and renewal of our lives in Jesus' name.

Change Your Focus

Don't allow situations to overwhelm you. God made you to overcome situations by keeping your focus on Kingdom things. What we focus on the most will be amplified the most in our lives. Situations do not demand your time, thoughts, energy, and emotions, but the Kingdom does!

> *But they that wait upon the LORD shall renew [their] strength.* (Isaiah 40:31)

Could that word "wait" mean waiting/serving like a waiter does that serves tables instead of waiting as if you are waiting on a bus? While you utilize patience, waiting on your change to come, you continue to wait (serve) Him because in doing so, your strength will be renewed. Job said, *I will wait until my change come.* (Job 14:14) David said, *I cried out to the Lord and He heard my cry.* Overcome hardship by being distracted by righteousness (serving God by serving others). For the next few days, I ask that you proclaim each morning, noon, and evening the following several times throughout the day: *Many [are] the afflictions of the righteous: but the LORD delivereth him out of them all.* (Psalms 34:19)

Times of Testing

Times of testing come, not to uncover our ignorance, but to solidify the things that we have been taught–to bring full assurance that the things that we have learned are sound, steadfast, and secure. Until all that we believe in is tested, we don't truly understand the magnitude or magnificence of what we believe. We simply utter phrases without conviction and share clichés void of experiences that validate them. Oh, how blessed is the man or woman who knows why they believe what they believe! Can a person be blessed in the midst of a test? Yes, we can be blessed in the middle of a crisis. These are the seasons when what we think becomes what we know!

Could it be that the thing you thought would take you out only serves to bring you in more? That which you thought would disqualify you, miraculously qualifies you. The very thing some thought would kill you and extinguish your flame only made you stronger and caused your passion to burn much hotter. Your crisis can become the fuel for your greatest breakthroughs, pushing you, challenging you, upsetting you, but ultimately helping you. Somehow, you can come to understand that the crisis only took from you what you did not need and only separated you from those who did not count toward your future. It only provoked you in the direction of your destiny. Passivity, indecision, and the luxury of procrastination were snatched from you the moment crisis came knocking at your door. Though you wouldn't have ordered it, somewhere deep inside, in a place almost untouched by conscious thought, praise is being birthed. Somehow you know that God is taking you to a place of total trust, without condition and without compromise, where you are just satisfied to know Him and let Him know you. Maybe that's what He's been after all along anyway.

The problem is that we are not always able to handle the truth He wants to give us. Most often, we are not able to fully comprehend what He is saying. A sign of maturity is developing the ability to hear what Jesus is trying to tell us rather than trying to get Him to join our own way of looking at things. He tends to get us to a point of maturity by taking us through situations that bring us to the place where we become very receptive to what He is saying to us.

Allow me to share something with you about the truth. What I mean by the truth is that we sometimes don't want to face a situation or even ourselves. Sometimes, truth can be so strong that if you were to tell a person the raw truth of a matter concerning themselves, they would have a meltdown. You can plug the cord of a radio in an electrical outlet and the radio will literally melt down because too much power is coming from the electrical outlet. What was needed was an "adapter" to be placed between the electrical outlet and the radio to convert the right voltage of power. If God or someone else were to present us with the truth, we would experience a similar meltdown. Oftentimes, we cannot handle the increase voltage. Therefore, the Lord provides us with adapters so that we are able to handle His truth. Jesus conveyed truth through parables, representative principles (In the absence of something God wants us to understand, He gives us something we do understand so that we can draw a comparison and comprehend what it is He is trying to tell us), and experience.

What you don't get by revelation, you get by situation. There are truths that Jesus wants you to grasp by revelation, but if you don't, you will understand through experience. Jesus is the ultimate teacher and He will not let us "graduate" without passing the test. Out of love, He will do what it takes for us to "get it", and that is usually where experience comes into play. After feeding five thousand, Jesus sent the multitude away, then told His disciples to get in a boat and start toward another city across the water. Within no time, they were in the middle of a raging storm. Why would Jesus send His disciples into a storm? Remember, they had missed the significance of feeding of five thousand. Mark says, *For they considered not the miracle of the loaves: for their heart was hardened.* (Mark 6:52) As a teacher, Jesus wasn't going to let His students move on until they were ready, and since they didn't understand through revelation, they were going to have to understand through experience. A "hardened" heart is not an evil heart. A hardened heart is one that is not illuminated. The disciples only failed to get (see and understand) what they were supposed to get out of the miracle of the loaves and fishes. To make matters worse, the disciples didn't even realize that they had failed to grasp what Jesus was trying to tell them. They didn't get it, and they didn't get that they didn't get it! Jesus gave them two clues about their condition, but that didn't help either.

CLUE #1 – Jesus told His disciples to go across the lake while He went up the mountain. This let them know that He was not going in the same direction.

CLUE #2 – Jesus put His disciples in the boat at twilight. So the further they got away from Him, the darker it was going to become.

The disciples rowed all night against the wind. Peter, the experienced fisherman, didn't need Jesus' help – or so he thought. Rowing with all of their human strength against the contrary winds was getting them nowhere. What we don't get by revelation we will get by situations, and life becomes a parable.

The fact is you can never out-row contrary winds. We have been in situations where God was saying one thing and yet, we wanted to pursue something else. Sometimes, there's a time for subtraction and development rather than growth and multiplication. Back in the boat, Peter finally got tired. About that time, Jesus came walking by on the water. Notice that the bible says Jesus *would have passed them by.* (Mark 6:48) He would have walked right past them because He will never follow or join any man's vain attempts against contrary winds. We follow Jesus, never the reverse. When the disciples recognized Him, acknowledged their need of Him, and invited him into the boat, they were immediately at the other side of the lake. (Matthew 14:22-34) The parable of the loaves and fishes and the storm was the same. What you have in your hands will not get you through unless you invite Jesus into the equation. You can't do it on your own. You must ask Jesus to be involved. The disciples didn't get it with the loaves because they were too busy congratulating each other on what a great job "they" had done. They were probably happy getting into the boat, thinking, "Wow, what a great time we had tonight. Did you see me flowing in the anointing, breaking bread like that?" They didn't get it and they didn't get that they didn't get it. But Jesus, being the Teacher, wouldn't let them move on until they got it!

The awareness of our lack tells us we are about to go somewhere. You don't notice missing keys until you are ready to go somewhere. This produces a seeking that intensifies the closer you are to your time of departure. In our crisis, we can become acutely aware of where we are at loss or lack. This awareness and subsequent seeking brings us to the point of truth, the point of becoming aware of things unknown or forgotten. We cannot get to the next level without putting it all in Jesus' hands.

What are you fighting for?

The Word instructs us to *contend for the faith.* (Jude 1:3) What we've come to realize is that it's not that I'm fighting to get something, but I'm fighting to keep the revelation that I've already got it! In saying that, it's not that I fight to keep the promise, but to keep the revelation that I already have everything I need through the finished work of Jesus Christ.

Usher in Change

In the church, there are supposed to be differences but not division. The church contains a unity of diversity, not a unity of conformity. If the church is to function properly, there must be different types of congregations. In the physical body, the most healthy heart will still die without healthy lungs, kidneys, and other vital organs. The same is true of the church. The different organs in the body do not compete with one another unless there is Cancer in the body. Cancer is basically made up of cells that determine that they are going to grow without regard to the rest of the body. Self-centered congregation and/or people that promote their own growth without regard to the rest of the church could likewise be called cancerous in the body of Christ. When Jesus prayed for His church, He prayed that she would be *perfected in unity, that the world may know **that Thou didst send me**.* (John 17) The world will not believe the gospel until it sees the church in unity. The church will not come into its perfection or maturity until it comes into unity. True unity will not come through compromise or political agreements between the leaders of different camps. In the Lord's prayer for the unity of His people, He declared how it would come: *The glory which thou hast given me, I have given to them; that they may be one, just as we are one.* When the Lamb enters, all the elders will cast their crowns at His feet. The church will never become what it was called to be until the attention is off of the church and back unto the Lord. When we glorify Christ, that ushers in change. John is the perfect model for new covenant ministry. His whole purpose was to point to Jesus and prepare the way for Him. He was willing to decrease and let Jesus increase. That is the true purpose of all ministries--to point to Jesus, prepare the way for Him, and then be willing to decrease in our own authority with people as their relationship grows with Him.

Take Heed

Wherefore let him that thinketh he standeth take heed lest he fall. (1 Corinthians 10:12)

We can become so sure of a thing (outside of God) that we begin to ease up on our vigilance and sobriety. When we become too sure sometimes, we become careless and that's when the adversary creeps in through a crack. I want you to be vigilant and sober, and on the lookout for any sign of unbelief, fear, and doubt. Then cast it down in the name of Jesus.

What is Faith?

Faith believes God can, God will, and God has done it. If you believe you have received it, you shall have it. Should God give you His word, you can thank Him by saying, "God *has* healed me; He *has* already done it!" Many believers merely expect to be healed. Expectation regards things in the future, but faith deals with the past. If we really believe, we shall not wait for twenty or one hundred years, but shall rise up immediately and say, "Thank God, I have received it. Thank God, I am clean. Thank God, I am well." A perfect faith can therefore proclaim God can, God will, and God has done it.

Faith works with "is" and not "wish". Here is a simple illustration. Suppose you preach the gospel and one professes that he has believed in that which you preach. Ask him whether he is saved, and should his answer be, "I wish to be saved", then you know this reply is inadequate. Should he say, "I will be saved", the answer is still incorrect. Even if he responds with, "I think I shall definitely be saved", something is yet missing. But when he answers, "I am saved", you know the flavor is right. If one believes, then he is saved. All faith deals with the past. To say, "I believe I shall be healed" is not true faith. If he believes, he will thank God and say, "I have already received my healing."

Grab hold of these three affirmations: God can, God will, and God has. When man's faith touches the third stage, whatever we ask for in faith is already done!

Build Better

Except the LORD build the house, they labour in vain that build it: except the LORD keep the city, the watchman waketh but in vain. (Psalms 127:1)

What struck me the most about this verse is that came while I was sitting drawing prints for a house, I stopped to reflect upon the Word and it spoke volumes to me. Throughout our lives, we are forever trying to build something for ourselves. But no matter how hard we try and what we attempt to build, whether it's a relationship, business, or ministry, if God is not in it, we are wasting our time.

What If?

Jesus said unto him, If thou canst believe, all things [are] possible to him that believeth. And straightway the father of the child cried out, and said with tears, Lord, I believe; help thou mine unbelief. (Mark 9:23-24)

Here's a man that actually believed but in the midst of his emotions and heat, being so attached to the very thing he believed God for, he asked the Lord to help him in his unbelief. In other words, we believe God for things that mean so much to us that in the midst of believing, hoping, and waiting, our hearts sometimes say, "What if?" If you have experienced that, I want you to know that you are not alone. The reason your heart may respond like this isn't because you don't believe, it's just that we want it so much and in wanting it so much, we wonder if there's a chance that we won't get it. I have had many days with these "what ifs". Jesus periodically mentioned to His disciples that He would be betrayed and crucified at different stages in His ministry. But as we get closer to that actual event, we now see Him in the garden praying, crying, and sweating. The closer He got to the actual event, the more it would cross His mind. Now, we see Him in the garden speaking as a man, *the spirit indeed* [is] *willing, but the flesh* [is] *weak.* (Matthew 26:41) I'm glad the writer included this in scripture. That's like saying, 'Look Father, I believe you in all things, but now that we are closing in to the point, my (natural) mind is beginning to consider this very thing.

109

The spirit is willing, but the flesh is weak.' I was looking at some of the things that the Word of God says concerning praying and believing.

Jesus reminded us through several passages that when praying, we have to believe and not doubt. (Mark 11:23, Matthew 21:21) James 1:6 goes on to say that he who doubts is like wavering on the sea. We have to be careful when doubt comes to our mind. Just as we confronted these physical desires and lust by the Word, let us also confront these doubts whenever they surface. The Word goes on to say in Luke that there appeared an angel unto Him from heaven to strengthen Him (Jesus). Now if the Lord went through this, you know we will also. Don't allow anyone to tell you that when you think, "What if?" that it is a sign of unbelief. No, it's a sign of honesty. When we are honest, we set the stage for God to strengthen us. He will send us an angel to strengthen us, as well. So I say to you if you are in a last hour of believing, praying, hoping, enduring and going through, that Jesus is on your side. So let's come against those thoughts of "what ifs" with the Word. We have asked God through prayer so therefore, we will believe Him totally by speaking as if it has already been granted.

You Have All You Need

Just as the widow with the pot of oil (1 Kings 17) did not realize what she had at her disposal was all that was needed for her situation. I want you to know that you have all that you need as well. The widow did not realize she had something that was so significant until crisis came into her life. Without the crisis, she would have never realized the value of what she had.

Wherein ye greatly rejoice, though now for a season, if need be, ye are in heaviness through manifold temptations: That the trial of your faith, being much more precious than of gold that perisheth, though it be tried with fire, might be found unto praise and honour and glory at the appearing of Jesus Christ. (1 Peter 1:6-7)

Crisis does not always signify that you did something wrong. For a believer, it also signifies God's desire to bring you into some things; bring some things out of you that you didn't realize were in you. The widow with the pot of oil had what she needed, but she didn't know until crisis showed up. The creditor (Satan) showed up for her sons.

And David was greatly distressed; for the people spake of stoning him, because the soul of all the people was grieved, every man for his sons and for his daughters: but David encouraged himself in the LORD his God. (1 Samuel 30:6)

Do not be discouraged; be as David and encourage yourself. Don't rely on anyone other than God and what He has given you. 1 Samuel 30:6 states that David was distressed, but he encouraged himself in the Lord his God. Verse 7 goes on to say that God told David AFTER he encouraged himself that he would pursue and overtake his enemies AND (there's always an extra when God is in the equation) and RECOVER ALL!

God may allow the crisis into your life to reveal to you that you have something God can use and you have all that is needed to get you the full victory in the situation. Allow your crisis to give birth to worship, trust, faith and development. Faith is what pleases God, worship brings you closer to Him and in doing so, you receive encouragement and strength. Trust shows that you are not looking at the circumstances, but instead you are looking at the solution, which is Jesus Christ, the author and finisher of our faith. (Hebrews 12:2)

Triumph over your crisis by encouraging yourself in the Lord. Pursue your enemies with the Word and your faith walk and without fail, RECOVER ALL!

Walking Confidently in God

We all have things that we struggle with, things we know God doesn't want in our lives forever. Lord knows we may have tried (works of faith) everything we can think of to overcome them, but yet we still struggle with them. I believe God at times allows us to go through such dilemmas so that when we come to the end of ourselves and see we cannot do it, that's when He says, "I told you. My grace is sufficient. Now stand back and see the salvation of the Lord." Worrying and focusing on those things, which we don't have the power and strength to overcome, won't change a thing. Why not just keep the desire to want to change, be delivered, and trust Him to come through? In the midst of continuing to have things we struggle with, we have to refuse to go crazy trying to do what we cannot. So instead, let's walk in confidence, knowing God sees it and has committed Himself to complete and perfect it. Attend to what you can handle, such as our conduct, worship, and service to the Lord. Before you know it, it will be gone away because the Word says, *I [Christ] have overcome the world* (John 16:33) on our behalf. Sometimes we have to wait longer in one area in order to see other manifestation. Your healing, deliverance, and life was predestined before the foundation of the world; it's just a matter of those things coming to you. Paul was excellent at this; he struggled with a thorn in his flesh, which he took to God and continued on, even while it remained. The enemy wants us to look at everything, but Jesus. Do the opposite!

Fear Isn't an Option

When Jesus therefore had received the vinegar, he said, It is finished: and he bowed his head, and gave up the ghost. (John 19:30)

According to the book of John, the last words that Jesus uttered were, "It is finished." What did He have reference to? The work given to him by the father and the works of Satan. The Word states that the son of man was manifested to destroy the works of Satan. We know that some of the works of Satan are to kill, steal, and destroy. (John 10:10) He attempts to kill anything worth killing. He attempts to destroy anything worth destroying. His beef isn't with the wicked. His beef is with God and what belongs to God; his people! This is why your peace, joy and confidence are always under attack. The world didn't give it to you; your Father did. He whose mind is stayed on the Lord, He will give him perfect peace (Isaiah 26:3); a peace that surpasses human understanding. (Philippians 4:7) The enemy doesn't desire to see you with peace. The Word teaches us that the joy of the Lord is our strength. (Nehemiah 8:10) The world doesn't give us joy; our joy comes from the Holy Spirit. The world doesn't give us confidence. Our confidence is in Christ. We have died so that Christ may live in us. Therefore, we don't see ourselves the way the world sees us. No, we see ourselves through the eyes (Word) of the living God. The Lord doesn't want us to have poor opinions and views about ourselves. Remember, what a man thinketh in his heart, so is he. So how do we think? We think with the mind of God. *For who hath known the mind of the Lord that he may instruct him? But we have the mind of Christ.* (1 Corinthians 2:16) Thinking like Christ demands that we have confidence in ourselves since we are new creatures in Christ, a chosen generation, a royal priesthood, a holy nation, a peculiar people. The verse goes on to say, *...that ye should shew forth the praises of him who hath called you out of darkness into his marvellous light* (1 Peter 2:9).

Come from behind those walls! Show forth the light that you know is in you!

The dictionary states that confidence is a state of self-assurance. The things that God has said about you, you can be more than sure that it's all true. If you feel insecure at the moment, know for sure that it is not God, but instead the enemy. Please look at Philippians 1:6 *...Being confident of this very thing, that he which hath begun a good work in you will perform* [it] *until the day of Jesus Christ:* If people don't understand you, it's their lost. God understands you, but He wants you to understand you through His eyes. Many times, it's not that people misunderstand us, but we misunderstand ourselves. Instead of seeing ourselves through the eyes of God, we are still entangled with old images, memories, and experiences concerning our lives.

And it came to pass, when they had brought them forth abroad, that he said, Escape for thy life; look not behind thee,

116

neither stay thou in all the plain; escape to the mountain, lest thou be consumed. (Genesis 19:17)

But his wife looked back from behind him, and she became a pillar of salt. (Genesis 19:26)

We read the story of Lot and see that they were instructed to leave Sodom and Gomorrah and to not to look back. For some reason, Lot's wife had a problem with following instructions. She looked back and was turned into a pillar of salt. What was it about this sister that led her to not obey sound counsel? Maybe she was so accustomed to the lifestyle of that city. Maybe she was accustomed to being comfortable in an uncomfortable situation because it had existed so long in her life. Whatever the reason, it cost the woman her life simply because she couldn't forget the things that were behind her and press forward. The Lord is asking us to move forward and not look back. That means that we have to let go of all those things that keep us down. We have to let go of all of those things that keep us in bondage. Letting go includes severing ourselves from the memories and emotions attached to them. Letting go and pressing forward means that we let go to the degree as if it never even happened. He wants us to move past the hurt, rejection, insecurity, doubt, and fears. In moving past them, we are letting go and never need to look back again. He didn't want Lot's wife to look back because the Lord had already pronounced judgment on that city. The only thing that was behind her was destruction. God wants to destroy those things that are behind us. He wants to destroy those memories, feelings, and things that keep us weighed down and in bondage. The things of the past that have harmed you, whether it was a relationship or loss of a loved one, the Lord wants you to move past that. He wants to destroy the very things that attach you those experiences. The things that cause you to suffer; the things that cause you to cry; the things that cause you to feel insecure; the things that cause you to wall yourself in to your own self-made prison. Experiences of our past shouldn't cause us to suffer. The experience shouldn't have an impact on your life to the point where you are incapable of enjoying life to its fullest extent in God.

For every battle of the warrior [is] *with confused noise, and garments rolled in blood; but* [this] *shall be with burning* [and] *fuel of fire.* (Isaiah 9:5)

Once again, Jesus said it was finished. He suffered and died for us so that we wouldn't have to suffer. *But he was wounded for our transgressions, he was bruised for our guilt and iniquities: the chastisement* [needful to obtain] *peace and well-being for us was upon Him, and with the stripes* [that wounded] *Him we are healed and made whole.* (Isaiah 53:5 AMP) You don't have to suffer any longer. He did it all! Acknowledge, accept, and receive it right now in Jesus' name.

The Key to Victory

We are not to complain and grumble about anything. Salvation is by and through Jesus alone. Stop trying to serve and please God through your own works of the flesh because it only frustrates you. Sanctification is a work of the Holy Spirit. Be patient and trust that God will work out all the undesirable things in our lives. Don't be hard on yourself because you struggle or have undesirable things about you. We become frustrated because we at times try to please God by works of the flesh, when God says that we are already (in spite of flaws) the righteousness of God through Christ Jesus. (Philippians 3:9) Therefore, righteous standing with God comes through Jesus alone and not works (deeds) of the flesh. Striving to be righteous and sanctified by our own attempts places us in bondage of the law all over again. The Lord says, *Stand fast therefore in the liberty wherewith Christ hath made us free, and be not entangled again with the yoke of bondage.* (Galatians 5:1) That yoke is the law and our personal striving through the flesh to please God. It only drives us crazy because we learn in time, that we don't have the strength to be as God desires us to be; we have to look to the One that does have the strength—Jesus Christ! Sin shall not have dominion for we are not under law, but grace. Yes, we may sin, but sin shall not rule us because we are not under law (works of the flesh) but under grace. If we simply follow the guiding of the Spirit of God, we will not fulfill the lust of the flesh. (Galatians 5:16) So the key to victory is by looking to Him alone and following His Spirit's guiding. The Spirit of the Lord will purge and sanctify in His way and His timing.

Be Still

Be still, and know that I am God: I will be exalted among the heathen, I will be exalted in the earth. (Psalms 46:10)

We are to be obedient, humble, loving, teachable and full of the joy of the Lord. Stop fighting the wrong battles that don't belong to you. Trust God and the fact that He's in control of all things and He knows what He is doing. Forget about what others are doing right or wrong, and focus on what God has before you. The enemy will create distractions before you so that you can become overwhelmed by what's going on. This causes you to wage battle against the wrong things, but when you battle, you battle against the vessel (brethren) rather than what's driving the vessel (Satan). While you're busying yourself with battles, you are neglecting your post (calling). Let those things go and fulfill your service to God. Refrain from judging, criticizing and accusing others, even when they are wrong. Judgment is reserved for God alone. Our assignment is to intercede and complete our assigned tasks. I know it hurts to see people being used and hurting themselves, but God says in His Word that in the last days, many false prophets, apostles and teachers will arise and deceive, but we are not to be overwhelmed by it. God's will is that you fear not in these times, but know that He is God.

Binding Heavy Burdens

But [like a boxer] *I buffet my body* [handle it roughly, discipline it by hardships] *and subdue it, for fear that after proclaiming to others the Gospel and things pertaining to it, I myself should become unfit* [not stand the test, be unapproved and rejected as a counterfeit]. (1 Corinthians 9:27 AMP)

Take my yoke upon you, and learn of me; for I am meek and lowly in heart: and ye shall find rest unto your souls. For my yoke is easy, and my burden is light. (Matthew 11:29-30)

Just as Paul said that he brings his body under control, we have to do the same thing when dealing with the stress of life. God has given us power over all the power of the enemy and nothing he attempts to destroy you with will or can prosper.

When you sense heaviness upon you, discern immediately that it comes from the world and it is not the will of God. God may place a burden upon our hearts, but not heaviness; there's a big difference. Jesus talked about how the Scribes and Pharisees would bind heavy burdens upon the shoulders of others. (Matthew 23:3-4) We know that when He does place a heavy hand upon us, it's always for our good. Walk, labor, and rest in the peace that Jesus gave you. Jesus never told us it's our responsibility to save and carry the burdens of the world; He did that. Our job is to be faithful and obedient to the will of God. There's also a joy that comes from doing the will, laboring, and being a faithful servant. Don't let the world or the church bind heavy burdens on you that the Lord Himself didn't place there.

Wasted Time

The time I wasted is my biggest regret,

Spent in the wrong places; I will never forget.

Just sitting and thinking about the things I have done,

The crying, the laughing, the hurt and the fun,

Behind a wall of emptiness I allowed to be built.

I am trapped in my body, just wanting to run,

Back to my youth, with its laughter and fun.

But the chase is over and there's no place to hide.

Everything is gone, including my pride.

With reality suddenly right in my face,

I am scared alone and stuck in this place.

Now memories of the past flash through my head,

And the pain is obvious by the tears that I shed.

I ask myself why and where I went wrong,

I guess I was weak when I should have been strong.

Living for the world and the wings I had grown,

My feelings were lost, afraid to be shown.

As I look at my past, it's easy to see,

the fear that I had, afraid to be me.

I would pretend to be rugged, so fast and so cool,

when actually I've lost, like a blinded fool.

I am getting too old for this tiresome game,

of acting real hard with no sense of shame.

It's time that I change and get on with my life,

fulfilling my dreams for a family and a wife.

What my future will hold, I do not completely know,

but the years that I have wasted are starting to show.

I just live for the day when I'll get a new start,

and the dreams I still hold deep in my heart.

I hope I can make it, I at least have to try,

because I'm heading toward death, and I don't want to die.

Oh wretched man that I am. Who shall deliver me from the body of this death?

I thank God through Jesus Christ our Lord for when he breathed his last breath

because the death, burial and resurrection of the Lord Jesus Christ

put this death thing to rest and gave me a new life.

So as I reflect back to all the time that I've wasted,

revelation allows me to see this thing called grace.

Although I made bad choices and things,

while I was still tripping, God was making my wings.

He allowed me to go through so much, through His permissive will,

because when the word came to me back then, I didn't want to chill.

In spite of my sin and rebellion,

He covered me anyway,

and the mercy and love of God brought me through each day.

Here I stand now, saved, delivered and set free,

blessed with every spiritual blessing in Heaven; it's good to be me!

The wings that He made me allow me to soar,

to soar above all circumstances, and my confidence is sure.

Confidence in my Jesus, and never in my flesh.

Although I lost many years of my life,

I now have it more abundantly through Jesus, My Christ.

"Was time really wasted?" is the question I ask.

Eternity

September 27, 2009

Made in the USA
Charleston, SC
26 December 2011